To

_____

From

_____

Date

_____

GOD IN
Every Moment

One-Minute Devotions
for Every Day

God in Every Moment: One-Minute Devotions for Every Day
Copyright © 2018 by DaySpring
First Edition, January 2018

Published by:

DaySpring

P.O. Box 1010
Siloam Springs, AR 72761
dayspring.com

Bible verses were taken from the following translations:

ESV: Scripture quotations taken from the ESV Bible® (The Holy Bible, English Standard Version®) copyright ©2001 by Crossway Bibles, a publishing ministry of Good News Publishers. Used by permission. All rights reserved.

THE MESSAGE: Scripture quotations from The Message. © Eugene Peterson. Permission from NavPress

NKJV: Scripture from the New King James Version. Copyright © 1982 by Thomas Nelson, Inc.

NLT: Scripture quotations are taken from the Holy Bible, New Living Translation, copyright © 1996, 2004, 2007 by Tyndale House Foundation. Used by permission of Tyndale House Publishers, Inc., Carol Stream, Illinois 60188. All rights reserved.

TLB: © The Living Bible. Taken from the Living Bible with permission from Tyndale House Publishers, Inc., Wheaton, IL.

Written by Bonnie Jensen
Designed by Jessica Wei
Typesetting by Greg Jackson of thinkpen.design

Printed in China

Prime: 71931
ISBN: 978-1-68408-222-3

And we know that all things work together
for good to those who love God, to those who
are the called according to His purpose.
ROMANS 8:28 NKJV

You are a miracle of God's making. Your unique purpose in this world is being worked out by His hand and heart every single day. The difference you're created to make is as finely and individually stitched as your very being. It will bring change to the lives of others, joy to you, and glory to Him.

Father, let me be aware of Your presence
in my day and in my decisions, knowing
that You're guiding me into my purpose.

JANUARY 2

How precious it is, Lord, to realize that
You are thinking about me constantly!
PSALM 139:17 TLB

It's so encouraging to get a surprise text, phone call, card, or letter, because they *all* send the same spirit-lifting message: someone is thinking about me! Now ponder the truth that God thinks about you *constantly*. What is it that initiates His moment-by-moment awareness of you? *Love*. He loves you so much that He can't—and won't—take His mind off of you. You're far too valuable to Him to neglect, *any* time of *any* day.

Lord, thank You for Your constant, loving attention. Help my heart to be encouraged every day by the thought of You thinking about me.

*You chart the path ahead of me and tell me where to
stop and rest. Every moment You know where I am.*

PSALM 139:3 TLB

Everything you go through has meaning.
Every moment of your life holds purpose.
When you surrender fully to God's intimate
navigation of your path, your steps become
more sure as you become more trusting of
His leading. He knows where you are at all
times—and He knows exactly where you need
to be at every part of your journey.

*Father, today I want to trust more, listen
closer, and follow the path You've chosen
for me with a fully surrendered heart.*

*And so the Lord has paid me with His blessings, for
I have done what is right, and I am pure of heart.*
PSALM 18:24 TLB

The right things you do today can only come
from a heart transformed by pure love.
When we realize the helplessness of our
human capabilities and the power of God's
perfect love to influence our actions, lives
are touched and changed for good. Smiles,
words, a hug, a helping hand—keep your eyes
open for moments to do what's right, and be
ready to receive the blessing of *joy*.

*Father, I'm Your vessel of pure love today. Use me
to do what is right and good for every life I touch.*

Now glory be to God, who by His mighty power at
work within us is able to do far more than we would
ever dare to ask or even dream of—infinitely beyond
our highest prayers, desires, thoughts, or hopes.
EPHESIANS 3:20 TLB

Life is a series of changes, brought about one
day at a time. We have to let go of every hurt,
every doubt, and every resentment we hold
about why God has brought us to the place we
are now. God's promises will pull us forward
and out of the muddy waters of *why*, and if
we lean into Him with faith and confidence,
the days ahead will be more amazing than we
can imagine.

Father, Your love and promises sustain
me today as I look forward with hope
and faith to the overwhelming goodness
You're bringing into my life.

JANUARY 6

That is why we can say without any doubt or fear,
"The Lord is my Helper, and I am not afraid
of anything that mere man can do to me."
HEBREWS 13:6 TLB

Even if our days begin with feelings of fear, we
can *still say*, "The Lord is my helper. I am not
afraid." Say it out loud and *listen*. His Word
is the truth. It has the power to overcome
the fear. No matter what you're facing in the
moment, the timeless truth is that you have
a helper—and He's not just any helper. He
holds the universe, *and you*, in the palm of
His hand.

Father, I believe You're my Helper in times of
uncertainty. Today I ask for the confidence to
defeat fear at every turn and walk unafraid
into the blessings You have for me.

Every good gift and every perfect gift is from above,
coming down from the Father of lights, with whom
there is no variation or shadow due to change.
JAMES 1:17 ESV

Today is a *good* gift. Perfect, because it comes from God and, if trusted to Him, is another step in becoming more *like* Him. Will there be opportunities to show His unconditional love? To follow the Spirit's leading in helping or encouraging someone? We live to learn how to *love*—moment by moment and day by God-given day.

Lord, thank You for the gift of another
day wrapped in Your perfect love.

Jesus Christ is the same
yesterday and today and forever.
HEBREWS 13:8 ESV

God loves you in every season,
yet His love is not seasonal;
He loves you in every circumstance,
yet His love is not circumstantial;
He loves you in every condition,
yet His love is not conditional.
ROY LESSIN

Father, my heart is so full when I stop
and contemplate how consistent and
constant Your love for me is.

*I will tell everyone how good You are,
and of Your constant, daily care.*
PSALM 71:15 TLB

Telling *yourself* how good God is at all times,
and on a daily basis, may be more important
than shouting it from the rooftops! It's too
easy to be discouraged by disappointments
and setbacks, which make us quick to forget
all God has done in the past. It also distracts
us from what He's doing in the *present*. God's
care is constant...continuous...persistent...
unchanging—and nothing, absolutely *nothing*,
can interrupt it.

*Lord, I will remember how good You are and
what You've done for me. Thank You for Your
constant care of me and all of my days.*

JANUARY 10

*O Lord my God, many and many a time You have
done great miracles for us, and we are ever in Your
thoughts. Who else can do such glorious things?*
PSALM 40:5 TLB

The miracle of your day is that it *means*
something. What seems ordinary has a part
in moving you to the extraordinary life God
has for you. Your heart's desire comes when
your heart is ready, and God is all about
readying hearts for the promises He's given.
The attention paid to detail in your life by the
One who created you is altogether *miraculous*—
and it's preparing you to see amazing things.

*Father, help me pay attention to all You're
doing with my heart today—thankful that not
a moment is wasted in the life You give.*

The joy of the Lord is your strength.
NEHEMIAH 8:10 TLB

How is it that the strength for our days come from the joy in our hearts? Simply put, joy and hope are intertwined. Joy brings a wonderful sense of well-being, the feeling that everything is going to be okay, the confidence that God is working things out, the *hope* needed to stand and smile. You don't have to tell yourself to be strong today—be *joyful*, and God's strength will carry you.

*Lord, fill me with Your joy today so that I
can stand, be strong, and smile through.*

JANUARY 12

Every moment You know where I am. You
know what I am going to say before I even
say it. You both precede and follow me and
place Your hand of blessing on my head.
PSALM 139:3–5 TLB

God's place in your life: He's before, behind, and beside you with a hand of blessing on your head. Take a moment to think about where the blessing goes from there—it pours over you, over every part of your life, onto everything you touch. Pay attention with all your heart. There are no coincidences. Not one. Whether it's difficult or delightful, God is in it. And you'll see, now or in the future… it's a blessing.

Father, I'm surrounded by You, and everything
in my day is blessed by Your hand. Help me see
things with my heart and know You're with me.

He has showered down upon us the richness
of His grace—for how well He understands us
and knows what is best for us at all times.
EPHESIANS 1:8 TLB

There's no earthly wealth comparable to grace: God's forgiveness and favor. One of the beautiful aspects of grace is that God understands us. He *knows* what's best and *wants* what's best for us at all times. We don't need to understand our circumstances; we need to believe that God is working them in our favor, because He "gets" us from the inside out. You're walking toward what's best for you—day by grace-filled day.

Father, I'm thankful for Your grace and
understanding, and I know Your heart wants
what's best for me every moment of every day.

*Be delighted with the Lord. Then He will
give you all your heart's desires.*

PSALM 37:4 TLB

Be as excited to face your day as God is to give
it to you! Be happy about Him, delighted to
serve Him, thrilled to think about what He's
going to give you—those things you hope for
deep down in your heart of hearts. There's
no stopping Him from blessing you when you
look forward to what He's doing in your life
and take pleasure in simply *loving* Him. It's a
sweet promise with the sweetest outcome.

*Lord, my heart desires You first and always. The
dreams You bring to life will only deepen my love
for You and fill me with greater gratefulness.*

Yes, I am the vine; you are the branches. Those who remain in Me, and I in them, will produce much fruit. For apart from Me you can do nothing.
JOHN 15:5 NLT

We're here to live, love, and learn, to grow in God and realize we're nothing without Him. Much fruit is much-needed in this world, and there's peace in letting God provide it through us. Some days our to-do list goes to the wayside for divinely driven purposes and we discover again how important it is to let go and *just trust*. God produces the fruit that falls on heaven's doorstep—and it's eternally sweet.

Father, help me to stay close to You so the good stuff grows in me. Let my fruit-bearing make a difference today.

January 16

The moment I called out, You stepped in;
You made my life large with strength.
PSALM 138:3 THE MESSAGE

In life there are moments of joy, moments of sorrow, and moments of crying out for rhyme and reason. Always and without fail we get God's *presence*, but oftentimes we wait to see His *purpose*. The great news? Strength gets bigger while we wait. Our lives become larger to make room for trust, faith, hope, and peace. That's the kind of stuff we want to be blessed with, because it makes every other blessing even better.

Lord, You are strength, peace, and purpose.
All that You allow in my life is bringing
about all that You've promised.

There is a right time for everything.
ECCLESIASTES 3:1 TLB

God's timing isn't always easy to understand, but it's always perfect. The time between our circumstance and His answer is a period of hope and trust. There are seasons when God asks us to trust Him wholeheartedly without seeing where we're going or knowing how we're growing. We can be sure that *everything* we face is filtered through God's hand—and He'll use it to make our hearts like His.

Father, fill me with hope today and
give me the courage to know that my
heart is becoming more like Yours.

It is God who arms me with strength,
and makes my way perfect.
PSALM 18:32 NKJV

It's a human thing to want our own way—and it's a *beautiful* thing to have a God who loves us unconditionally. He will not turn away from us even if we stumble, misstep, or fall on our journey. He watches our steps, allows our choices, and arms us with the strength to make our way back to Him. His way is perfect, as is His heart…and both are filled with love.

Lord, give me the strength to stay on
the path of Your perfect way.

*My grace is sufficient for you, for My
strength is made perfect in weakness.*
II CORINTHIANS 12:9 NKJV

The depth of God's grace will always surpass
the depth of our weaknesses. In truth,
His grace *has* no measure. It's deeper than
our deepest need and able to sustain us in
moments when we feel too weak to fight a
moment longer. His grace covers you, His
strength carries you—and the more you lean
in, the more you'll stand strong.

*Father, Your grace is all I need today
to overcome all I face or fear.*

Trust in Him at all times. Pour out your
heart to Him, for God is our refuge.
PSALM 62:8 NLT

It seems unnecessary to pour out our heart to God. After all, "The LORD sees every heart and knows every plan and thought" (I Chronicles 28:9). The pouring out isn't for Him; it's for us. Confessing our need helps us realize our need for Him. We can't handle our days with a closed-door policy on our hearts. We have to pour out *everything*—from pressures to praise—because when we let weaknesses out, His strength comes in.

Father, my heart is open and surrendered
to You. Be my rest and refuge today.

*You go before me and follow me. You place
Your hand of blessing on my head.*
PSALM 139:5 NLT

Live by moments. The only One who can go ahead of you already has—and He's blessed the way. Lists and schedules can do a lot to keep you on track, but God has done *everything* to keep you peaceful, hopeful, happy, and whole. There's a no-fail policy on His partnership and promise to bless your life—and it went into effect the moment you were born.

*Lord, help me to be in the moment and
thankful today. I have peace knowing
You've gone ahead to bless the way.*

Don't be anxious…God will take care of your
tomorrow too. Live one day at a time.
MATTHEW 6:34 TLB

Life. You can't do it ahead of time, and you can't do it over. It's *right now* stuff. The task in front of you, the people you're with, the day God is giving you—give all of yourself to it. What doesn't get done isn't fault or failure; it's surrender and success. Without worry, you let God have control and simply *live*.

Father, You orchestrate my day with love
and care. Let me let go of it with joy.

*Your goodness and unfailing love will
pursue me all the days of my life.*
PSALM 23:6 NLT

All day, every day, God's love and goodness
are coming at you. *Pursuing* you. Where you
are, He *is*...with good plans, good-for-
you experiences, and good-for-your-heart
opportunities to grow. Even when days feel
hard and leave questions, you're standing
smack-dab in the middle of the love that's
working everything together for something
really, really good.

*Lord, Your continuous, loving pursuit of me
is a reminder of how valuable I am to You.*

JANUARY 24

Be full of love for others,
following the example of Christ...
EPHESIANS 5:2 TLB

Loving others—*all* others—is sometimes a challenge. Then we stop for a moment and think about what Jesus did not because we're easy to love, but because He knew that only love could change us and save us. It's the one thing that should *never* have to be earned to be given. So let's fill our hearts with God's kind of love and live today loving others.

Lord, keep me mindful of Your perfect love
today so that I can give it to others generously.

*You saw me before I was born. Every day of my
life was recorded in Your book. Every moment
was laid out before a single day had passed.*
PSALM 139:16 NLT

We have a single priority every day: trust God
with the outcome. Plans come and go;
God stays. Distractions change our direction;
God never changes. Interruptions test our
peace and patience; God stands ready to
help us stay calm and respond with love. He
wrote today's page before we were born—
making every moment an opportunity to
magnify Him.

*Father, all my days are pages penned by Your
hand. Let those who read them see You.*

The LORD is my strength and shield.
I trust Him with all my heart.
PSALM 28:7 NLT

Where you are at this moment is no surprise to God. He knew every choice you'd make, and He knew those choices would bring you to this place in your life. Because He's always known where you'd be, He's already worked the pieces together for your good. Even if we step out of His perfect will, we step into His amazing grace—and love *always* leads us back to His best.

Lord, let my steps be led by Your love today,
and let my heart be in tune with Your will.

O Lord, You have examined my heart
and know everything about me.
PSALM 139:1 TLB

Every moment is breathed by the One who
knows everything about you. Not just the
favorite color, little habits, sound of your
laughter stuff, but the state of your heart. And
He doesn't glance—He examines. He searches
in detail to see the nature and condition of
the true you He created. What does He hope
to see? That you're ready to receive every
dream He deposited when He formed you in
the palm of His hand.

Father, let my heart be surrendered to You
and shaped into all You created me to be.

You have been with me from birth and have helped me constantly—no wonder I am always praising You!
PSALM 71:6 TLB

Your day is God-initiated, God-infused, and God-involved. He's in every minute, hoping you see the meaning in it. Because we live in an imperfect body and an imperfect world, things are going to happen to pull us away from the peace of God's control. But His constant presence offers us the power to stay in always-praising mode—by remembering that He stays in always-good mode.

Lord, Your presence is power in every moment of my day.

Nothing can ever separate us from His love...our
fears for today, our worries about tomorrow...
ROMANS 8:38 TLB

Even on days when your mind is cluttered
with fear and worry, love will make its way
in. It will find the smallest clearing and have
the biggest presence. Kick the cares aside
and focus on it. God is right in front of you,
that monumental love reaching out to hold
you close and whisper, "Let Me have them.
Every worry, every fear. I've got them—and
I've got *you.*

Father, my fears are no match for Your love
today. Thank You for being my refuge.

His compassions fail not. They are new every morning.
LAMENTATIONS 3:22—23 NKJV

Not once in a while or when He feels like it—God's tender, understanding, unwavering love is new the moment you open your eyes every morning. Mistakes? Forgotten. It's time to move forward unafraid. Love has whitewashed the day and God is ready to make it beautiful *through* you and *for* you.

Lord, a new day is a new reminder of Your
love and mercy toward me. I'm thankful
to move forward for Your glory.

*Every morning tell Him, "Thank You
for Your kindness," and every evening
rejoice in all His faithfulness.*
PSALM 92:2 TLB

There are days that begin spectacularly and days that begin by testing every ounce of our patience. No matter what happens at the starting line, a thankful heart can change how we feel at the finish line. It will inspire us to run through the ribbon at the end of the day, rejoicing in God's faithfulness, because there will *always* be moments to see it—and thankfulness will keep our eyes wide-open.

*Lord, I'm thankful for Your kindness and
amazed by Your faithfulness to me every day.*

Those who trust in the Lord are steady...
unmoved by any circumstance.
PSALM 125:1 TLB

Trust. It isn't easy in every circumstance. Believing God's love is present and prevalent in spite of what we see or go through will test our hearts at the deepest levels. But what we discover there are undeniable truths that God wants stirred up—His love is truer than what we see, stronger than anything we go through, and powerful enough to cut through the pain to the comfort found in Him alone.

Father, I trust You today to the depths of my
soul. In every circumstance, You are my all.

I will go before you and make the
crooked places straight.
ISAIAH 45:2 NKJV

The sun rises on a new day. Thoughts of what you have to do start racing through your mind. Mapped out, they look like lines going every which way. Then there's the good news— the *great* news. God's been here, straightening the crooked places…for bumps, His wisdom; for stumbles, His grace; for weakness, His strength. You win today, because God has paved the way.

Lord, I know You've gone before me and
made the way for a truly good day.

My purpose is to give life in all its fullness.
JOHN 10:10 TLB

To be full or completely satisfied on this earth is to be filled with the One who created it. God is wholeness in every sense of the word. If there's *anything* else we feel we need to enjoy the fullness of this life, we will never be truly satisfied. A full life was God's purpose in sending Jesus—His destiny was the cross, His purpose was love, and His reason was you.

Father, I pray my joy is in the fullness
of Your life and love today.

Don't worry about anything; instead,
pray about everything.
PHILIPPIANS 4:6 TLB

First pray, then do. Four tiny words that change the course of a day. Can you imagine following the admonishment in this scripture without fail? Don't worry…pray. God knew we couldn't do both at the same time, so He gave us the best and only way to defeat worry moment by moment: *talk to Me about it.*

Father, I know worries are wasted
opportunities to trust You. Today, let
all my cares become prayers.

My love won't walk away from you.
ISAIAH 54:10 THE MESSAGE

There are no perfect words or ways to soothe the pain of loss in life, but there is a perfect promise to carry us through. God—with love miraculous and magnificent—will never walk away. Even when it's hard to see Him through the pools of tear-filled eyes, He's there. Every tough-to-get-through moment, He's there. So when your heart is facing a difficult day, know that God's wide-open arms are facing you.

Father, thank You for Your powerful and present love.

If you follow Me...living light will flood your path.
JOHN 8:12 TLB

The moments in this day will not come again—be a light in each one you can. Wouldn't it be wonderful if God allowed us to turn back and see the "drops of light" we leave throughout the day? Following Him with every action, choice, and word floods our path with living light—making moments that add up to difference-making days.

Lord, let today be one that brings Your living light to others through me.

Always be joyful. Always keep on praying.
No matter what happens, always be thankful, for this
is God's will for you who belong to Christ Jesus.
I THESSALONIANS 5:16—18 TLB

Always is absolute—and joyfulness, prayerfulness, and thankfulness are absolute essentials of blessed days. The only way to be consistent in the good things is to stay close to the One who is always good. While we change with moods, circumstances, and struggles, God remains steadily in control—asking us to remain steadfast in trusting Him.

Father, I'll stay close and steadfast today,
trusting and thanking You always.

...You can show others the goodness of God, for He called you out of the darkness into His wonderful light.
1 PETER 2:9 NLT

You're called into God's wonderful light. Imagine closing your eyes and turning your face toward it like warm sunshine. It feels overwhelming, as it should. It's the very reason we're able to show God to the world. When we're mindful of the light that's in and around us, it shines on others—putting a spotlight on the incredible goodness of God.

Father, standing in the light
of Your presence is the best preparation
for showing others Your goodness.

You are good and do only good;
make me follow Your lead.
PSALM 119:68 TLB

Do-good moments can change the direction of our day and, in turn, brighten the day of the one receiving the goodness. It's a big deal to let God lead us in the little things. They add up. They multiply. They eventually squeeze out *our* way to make more room for *His* way. If we let God lead the moments, we see goodness rule the day.

Father, I give You my day—
help me to stay out of the way.

Show me the path where I should go, O Lord;
point out the right road for me to walk.
PSALM 25:4 TLB

I keep three words in front of me on my
writing desk: *Relax. Accept. Bless.* They guide my
day. If we believe God will show us the way,
we can *relax* and rest in Him. If things don't
happen when we hope they will, we must *accept*
it and continue to *bless*—give, be thankful, be
joyful, be Christlike. Being like Him takes
our mind off us...and the best things come
from that.

Father, as You show me the way I should
go, give me the wisdom to see it clearly.

It is God Himself who has made us what we are.
EPHESIANS 2:10 TLB

Today is an empty canvas. Paint it with moments that make God smile. When you were created, He put a unique combination of gifts in you. He knew exactly how you would color the world more beautifully. All that you are is a part of all that He is—and today's an opportunity to let it shine.

Lord, thank You making me in Your image, for Your glory.

*...We can be mirrors that brightly reflect the glory
of the Lord. And as the Spirit of the Lord works
within us, we become more and more like Him.*
II CORINTHIANS 3:18 TLB

More and more like Jesus. God is working
within us to make us *that* beautiful. It's hard
to imagine how bright the reflection of His
glory would become if we fully surrendered
to His handiwork. Almost as amazing is the
depth of love it takes to *not* give up on us
in spite of our weaknesses, shortcomings,
stubbornness—human things. Let's fill today
with mirror moments...and let Him make us
brighter than ever.

*Father, my desire is to be more like Jesus and a
brighter reflection of Your glory every day.*

I will praise You, for I am fearfully and
wonderfully made; marvelous are Your works,
and that my soul knows very well.
PSALM 139:14 NKJV

What God puts in us makes us who we are;
what we do with it makes us who we become.
Everything we need to live out our purpose is
stitched into the fabric of our dreams. God
knows what you hope for. Every moment of
every day He's rooting for you, fighting for
you. Days spent in hope bring you one day
closer to your heart's desires and the unique
and beautiful purpose within you.

Father, my praise is for You, my hope is in You,
and every desire I have is for Your glory.

Christ has given each of us special abilities—whatever
He wants us to have out of His rich storehouse of gifts.
EPHESIANS 4:7 TLB

You have gifts from the greatest Giver—and
they're given to you to do the greatest amount
of good. Today there will be moments to
engage the special things God wove into you
as an individual. He designed you to carry
His gifts to the places and people on the path
of your purpose. And your steps will leave a
trail of joy, smiles, encouragement, hope,
love, and strength.

Father, let me be a vessel of Your goodness
to those who cross my path today.

I will hope continually, and will
praise You yet more and more.
PSALM 71:14 NKJV

Our circumstances are temporary and our God is enough. There is reason to have continual hope because God is continually faithful—and if we look back, we can see why our hearts continually become deeper wells of praise. God doesn't turn His back on our moments, from the mundane to the monumental. He shines in both with the same love, provision, and grace.

Father, I'll look for Your love and grace in
the moments and praise You even more.

Love never gives up, never loses faith, is always
hopeful, and endures through every circumstance.
I CORINTHIANS 13:7 NLT

Some days, *never give up* sounds a little like *move*
a mountain. But the One who can and will move
mountains in our lives is holding us steady
with love that never fails. It's stronger than
what stands before us and mightier than the
mistakes we make. God's love is hopeful and
enduring—and your day is in its firm and
faithful hold.

Lord, thank You for love that cares for us
and keeps us every moment of the day.

FEBRUARY 17

*Whatever I am now it is all because God poured
out such kindness and grace upon me...*
I CORINTHIANS 15:10 TLB

By God's grace, every good thing we do is
in Him, for Him, and through Him. And
it's a good thing to sometimes reflect on
the transformation our hearts have gone
through by being "drenched" in the grace and
kindness of God. The beauty we embody now
is a heavenly light powered by love—and it's *all*
because of Him.

*Lord, make me a light for others today and
let them see the beauty of Your love.*

So cheer up! Take courage if you
are depending on the Lord.
PSALM 31:24 TLB

Courage cultivates trust in God. It's not always easy to keep being brave—unless we keep filling up with faith. When we downplay our doubts and lift up His truth, we get in the habit of depending on the Lord. The more we see Him come through with His promises and provision, the more we begin to trust and the more courageous we become.

Lord, I'll be happy and courageous today
because my heart depends on You.

...You have never forsaken those who trust in You.
PSALM 9:10 TLB

Never. That's how many times God will let us down if we trust in Him. Does it mean everything will play out exactly how we thought it would? Nope. Does it mean everything will unfold without a struggle? Not always. Does it mean everything is in His control and will happen for our greatest good and His greatest glory? YES. Undeniably, unquestionably, *yes.*

Father, I put my trust in You and believe in my heart that You won't leave me for a moment.

...Even before I was born, God had chosen me to be His and called me—what kindness and grace.
GALATIANS 1:15 TLB

You were chosen and called before you were born. God knew you would be His and that your heart's desire would be to fulfill the purpose He designed for you. Days aren't wasted. Even when it feel's they aren't meaningful and God isn't moving, know that they are because He *is*. Miracles happen in moments—and God's timing is perfect.

Father, thank You for choosing me and giving purpose to all my moments and days.

*...Be filled with His mighty, glorious strength
so that you can keep going no matter what
happens—always full of the joy of the Lord.*
COLOSSIANS 1:11 TLB

Grace is the beautiful reminder that God understands, forgives, and loves us—no matter what. Hold your head high today and *keep going*. Decide to be full of the joy of the Lord so you can be full of His mighty, glorious strength. Face the day and fill the moments with bravery and boldness, because God's got you in the arms of grace.

*Lord, Your grace is all I need today
to greet every moment with joy.*

*...God of mercy and grace, endlessly
patient—so much love, so deeply true...*
EXODUS 34:6—7 THE MESSAGE

God of mercy and grace, compassion and
favor, You see our day begin and at once
Your love is ignited. You know what will
happen every moment because You're *in*
every moment. Your plans are good and
our prayers are heard. You love us through
and through, sunrise to sunset. Your love
makes the moments count—and it's the most
beautiful part of who we are.

*Father, let Your love radiate from my
words and my actions today.*

...I chose you! I appointed you to go and produce lovely fruit always, so that no matter what you ask for from the Father, using my name, He will give it to you.
JOHN 15:16 TLB

God gives what is best, does what is most loving, and fulfills our heart's desires. He knows each one intimately because He put them there. He put them there to see them come to pass. Our true purpose is going to produce lovely fruit, inspire loving praise, and give incredible joy—one moment at a time.

Father, thank You for choosing me to bear fruit that will last forever.

He is close to all who call on Him sincerely.
He fulfills the desires of those who
reverence and trust Him…
PSALM 145:18—19 TLB

God sees your heart and hears your voice. He knows that trusting Him is one of the bravest things you do. He's working out your hopes and desires, and He knows that when He brings them to pass they'll bring a joy you've never felt before. Breathe in the moments today, smile, and know He's close—with all the comfort and courage you need.

Father, I trust You. I put my hope
and my day in Your hands.

God's way is perfect.
All the LORD's promises prove true...
II SAMUEL 22:31 NLT

Hope is powerful when it's put in the promises of God. As a matter of fact, it can't be defeated. Mistakes won't diminish it and circumstances won't extinguish it. Hope is fire in the soul and determination in the spirit. If you hold onto it today in spite of what you see or feel, you're going to invite the faithfulness of God—and He will *never* fail you.

Lord, my hope is in You alone, and my
heart holds on to Your promises.

...We are able to hold our heads high no matter
what happens and know that all is well, for
we know how dearly God loves us...
ROMANS 5:5 TLB

All is well because you are loved. You are
loved because you are priceless to God. No
matter what happens in the moments of your
day, His love for you is why you can hold
your head high and believe that everything is
going to be okay. Good things will be sweeter,
tough things will be easier, mistakes will be
forgiven—and the sun will set with Him loving
you as unconditionally as ever.

Father, my heart is at peace in Your love
and my day is blessed in Your hands.

The eyes of the Lord are watching
over those who fear Him,
who rely upon His steady love…
PSALM 33:18 TLB

There are moments we can't afford to miss…the heart-seeking moments that defy questions, cancel doubts, and defeat fear. The ways God shows His attentiveness in breathtaking, personal exchanges. *I see you—I know you—I hear you. I'm cheering for you, child, and not a second of your life escapes My sight.* When God reveals His presence, our hearts remember His promises and feel the indescribable joy of His love.

Lord, Your steady love brings the truest joy.
Open my eyes to see You reveal it.

...Nothing can ever separate us from God's love.
ROMANS 8:38 NLT

Nothing on this earth can stop God's love from reaching us when we need to see and feel it most...and thankfully, nothing will keep Him from showing it. He knows when we're at the end of our hope rope. Words, perfectly spoken or written; an out-of-the-blue act of kindness; the spotting of a favorite bird or the sun peeking through on a dreary day—they're little love notes saying, "I love you and I'm *here*...."

Father, help me see the little acts of love
You sprinkle throughout my day.

God is doing what is best for us....
HEBREWS 12:10 THE MESSAGE

God's best is yours because you are *His*. If you ever wonder what He's up to in your life, the answer is *whatever is best for you*. The steps He guides you to take, the people He brings across your path, the dreams that continue to stir your heart—He's moving everything into place for the best outcome, and it will always bring a greater revelation of His love and grace.

Father, Your best brings the greatest blessings.
I trust Your love and Your lead today.

Happy are those who are strong in the Lord,
who want above all else to follow Your steps.
PSALM 84:5 TLB

Happy and strong. That's *you*, following *Him*. There's no way to be stronger and no steps that are steadier. Following God is a matter of forfeiting our way for His. We often plow through the days with our agendas in mind, but it only takes a moment in the beginning to say, "God, I'm all Yours. Lead the way and I'll follow."

Lord, help me to live my day Your way.
My heart is surrendered to You.

Those who are wise—the people of God—shall
shine as brightly as the sun's brilliance…
DANIEL 12:3 TLB

Let your one-of-a-kind spirit shine today—
God's brilliant light through your life. It takes
putting the spotlight on those around you.
These are God-orchestrated relationships
and interactions in the moments of your
day. He's equipped you with gifts that will be
a blessing to other. The wisdom to see the
need, and be the light, will come from Him.

Father, give me the wisdom to be Your light
and love to everyone around me today.

...With God, everything is possible.
MARK 10:27 TLB

You can do anything through the One who gave everything for you. God holds nothing back when it comes to blessing you, and He doesn't take a day off or a moment's rest. You are His priority—and the power of His love can move mountains, calm storms, part seas, and realize dreams.

Father, give me the confidence to carry out my dreams and put my hope in the power of Your love.

...May those who love the Lord shine as the sun!
JUDGES 5:31 TLB

The sun will rise and *you* will shine today. Let those in need of a little hope see it in the light of your smile. Let those who long for a caring word hear it in the warmth of your voice. And let those needing brightness to chase the sadness find it in the One who lives in your heart.

*Lord, let my love for You be a
light for others today.*

You have made wide steps for my feet,
to keep them from slipping.
II SAMUEL 22:37 TLB

There's trust in stepping forward without fear. Our lives are a series of decisions to step in one direction or another. At times we won't see the path ahead. The sweet assurance we have is that God will keep us from slipping. If He has to widen the steps beneath our feet or catch us when we fall, He will.

Father, You are the rock beneath my
feet and the refuge for my soul.

...The joy of the Lord is your strength....
NEHEMIAH 8:10 TLB

Choose joy and stay strong. It only takes a short prayer to change a long day. God is working for you, moving the puzzle pieces into place, and He loves to see a smile on your face. A decision to be joyful floods your mind and your heart with hope—and the strength it brings will lift that hope even higher.

Lord, fill me with joy and hope, and be the strength of my heart today.

So we're not giving up. How could we! Even though on the outside it often looks like things are falling apart on us, on the inside, where God is making new life, not a day goes by without His unfolding grace.
II CORINTHIANS 4:16 THE MESSAGE

It's an inside job, making us new. It happens in the heart. It's where we first opened the door to let God in and felt the overwhelming relief of being loved completely. Everything we thought we knew about being good and loving others was overshadowed by His astounding grace. Today might look messy on the outside, but know that God is at work where it matters—so that the fruit of our lives will matter most.

Lord, let me walk in Your life-giving grace today and trust You with my whole heart.

*For I know the plans I have for you, says the
Lord. They are plans for good and not for
evil, to give you a future and a hope.*
JEREMIAH 29:11 TLB

God's plans for you are as special as you are.
They were thoughtfully designed to align with
your unique and wonderful wiring. But be
sure, they're going to be about spreading the
love. The one thing all God's plans have in
common? They're *good*—good for pointing
hearts to Him. His plans for each of us come
down to that one thing, repeated in the
moments that make up the days: love, love,
love.

*Father, Your love is always good and
all that matters. My hope for today
is to show it more and more.*

We should make plans—
counting on God to direct us.
PROVERBS 16:9 TLB

Our plans can be made, but God's plans will prevail. We wouldn't want it any other way. We might fall asleep with questions and wake up without answers, pressing through our days with tangled thoughts of what to do and what's next. Here's the truth: God's directing the moments. Count on it. Believe it because He believes in you—and He's faithfully guiding everything you do.

Father, I'm counting on You today and
believe You're directing every step.

Let every detail in your lives—words, actions,
whatever—be done in the name of the Master, Jesus,
thanking God the Father every step of the way.
COLOSSIANS 3:17 THE MESSAGE

You have a beautiful purpose in God—live it now! Live the details, the moments, the little things that, glued together, make a life—and make lives better. Be bold and brave enough to love when it's hard and be thankful when it's tough and you can't see how it's going to turn into something good. But *everything* done with a kind, loving, thankful heart is leading to good—your good from God's good.

Father, with a thankful heart, let me be
goodness, light, and love today.

The Lord will work out His plans for my life.
PSALM 138:8 TLB

It's going to be a good day! God is working out His plans for your life in all the best ways for all the best reasons. This is a journey of discovery for you, but He knows exactly what's coming and you can trust that it includes good-for-the-heart, beyond-measure blessings. Keep your heart thankful, your chin up, and your faith strong.

Lord, thank You for the good in my day and the love in Your plans.

*In everything you do, put God first, and He will
direct you and crown your efforts with success.*
PROVERBS 3:6 TLB

You're on your very own God-paved journey.
Enjoy the steps today! Don't overthink them;
simply live them with trust. Trust in His love
for you, His constant care of you, His joy
in seeing your joy. Peace is a provision that
comes with putting God first—and putting
Him first is the path to success.

*Father, I give You first place in all I do and
say today. Thank You for Your faithfulness.*

Make me understand what You want;
for then I shall see Your miracles.
PSALM 119:27 TLB

It's not a new prayer, to ask God for clear direction, yet it's a needed one. It should be our daily plea. The surest answer we will ever get on the path of His purpose is peace of heart. Ask Him for wisdom in the way to go, the choice to make, the road to take. He's listening—and forever faithful in answering.

Father, I want to go forward with peace in
my heart and see Your miracles in my life.

> *Love the Lord your God with all*
> *your heart, soul, and mind.*
> MATTHEW 22:37 TLB

Start the day with love. Before saying a word, say a prayer. *I love You, God.* Then begin. Love Him with all your heart and always first, and your heart will be in the right place for the rest of the day. When you *give* love, you *get* love, and from your Father that means eternal, gracious, boundless, all-encompassing, never-ending love—more than enough to spread generously on every life you touch.

Lord, I love You and give every moment of
my day to sharing Your love with others.

Be delighted with the Lord. Then He will
give you all your heart's desires.
PSALM 37:4 TLB

Delighted...happy...pleased. If our hearts
are surrendered and all-in when it comes to
loving God, being delighted with Him should
be an absolute joy! And on the heels of that joy
He gives us our heart's desires. There's beauty
in every part of that promise. The giving is all
God's and the blessing is all ours—and isn't
that just like our *magnificent* God.

Lord, my heart is delighted with you today
and thankful for Your promises.

*Out of His glorious, unlimited resources He will give
you the mighty inner strengthening of His Holy Spirit.*
EPHESIANS 3:16 TLB

There's no end to God's love and no limit to
His goodness. Like His love, God's *strength* is
unlimited—and it's all yours today. Whatever
your heart needs, His Spirit will give without
measure. Whatever you face today, He will
help you overcome. When you feel at your
weakest point, He will be there to pick you up.

*Father, Your boundless strength gives me
courage today as I put my hope in You.*

He fills my life with good things!…
PSALM 103:5 TLB

Start your day by looking at the good. Think of the good. Believe it's going to get even better. When God promises to fill your life with good things, get ready to be overtaken! His measure is more than you can ask or imagine. That's something to be happy about even though you can't fathom how amazing it will be.

Father, thank You for all You've given and for all that is yet to come.

*Always be humble and gentle. Be patient
with each other, making allowance for each
other's faults because of your love.*
EPHESIANS 4:2 NLT

There's always a way to make the best of
our day—even the ones that feel painfully
human with our struggles and stumbles and
broken hearts. With God's covering of love,
compassion, and forgiveness, we can stand
tall and stay strong through it all. And maybe
if we're feeling strong, we can help someone
else get back on their feet. Lifting a soul is a
great way to make the best of *any* day.

*Father, give me the wisdom to see the needs around
me and the strength to share Your light and love.*

…When dreams come true at last, there is life and joy.
PROVERBS 13:12 TLB

God is moving you toward your dreams. He knows each one because they align perfectly with the gifts He's given you. He wants your dreams to bring life and joy, so the timing is in His hands. Today might be another step on the journey, or it might hold what your heart has been waiting for. Either way, it's *God's* way—and that's always what is best for you.

Father, I put my dreams and their
timing in Your hand.

Be still, and know that I am God...
PSALM 46:10 NKJV

Being still is quietly trusting that God has the moments of our day in complete control. Nothing that happens is going to surprise Him in any way, so let's take a deep breath of faith and exhale the worry, the doubts, the questions. His answer is always, "I am your strength. I am your hope. I am your joy. I am your provider. I am *whatever you need*...."

Father, I will be still and trust in
Your constant care today.

*...I will bless you...and you will be
a blessing to many others.*
GENESIS 12:2 TLB

We are so blessed. Let's just start with love that has no end, no conditions. Then there's unspeakable joy and peace beyond understanding—it just pours over us when things go really wrong or get scary or fall apart. How do we contain all this divine goodness? We don't. We bless it away—to every person we see today who needs an ounce of heaven's help. Give, give, *give*. And watch your blessings keep coming.

*Father, I praise and thank You for the endless
blessings You give to me to give to others.*

...Fix your thoughts on what is true, and honorable, and right, and pure, and lovely, and admirable. Think about things that are excellent and worthy of praise.
PHILIPPIANS 4:8 NLT

Every moment brings a thought choice. We can think about what is good and praiseworthy, like God's incredible love for us and how it's *in* us to give *out*...or we can think about how unfair and unkind the world can be. Choosing the right thoughts can change the world's actions—and it starts with the love that changed *us*.

Lord, I choose to focus on Your love today
so the world will see Your light in me.

*...Trust in Him at all times. Pour out your
heart to Him, for God is our refuge.*
PSALM 62:8 NLT

Dare to trust God with all your heart. Give
Him the stuff you worry about, the clutter
keeping you awake at night, the distractions
throughout the day. Every care you carry
steals moments of peace that come from
God carrying you. He puts our life moments
in order for a reason—so we don't miss the
present, right-in-front-of-us cries for a love
that heals, a hope that holds, and a shelter
that stays.

*Father, let me be present in every
moment...for every heart and soul in
need of Your sheltering love.*

You love me so much! You are constantly so kind!...
PSALM 86:13 TLB

Kindness is how the heart gives love. We need to give big. Some days are tougher on our souls, when it might be a struggle to smile and we might have to dig deep to give anything good away. Do that, though. Dig deep. That's where God is, and He's the source of more than enough good stuff—the life-changing, eternity-etching kind of kindness that every heart needs.

Father, fill my heart with kindness so
I can fill my day with Your love.

...Let us stop just saying we love people; let us really love them, and show it by our actions.
I JOHN 3:18 TLB

If we put love into every action, we invite God into every moment. Sometimes the moments needing the most love land right in the middle of the stress and the mess and the heartache. That's when we breathe and believe—love isn't how we feel, and it isn't about us. It's about God *in* us, trusting us to show the world there's perfect love for the imperfect—*and here it is in front of you.*

Father, help me be an expression of Your perfect love today...moment by moment.

*Don't hide your light! Let it shine for all; let
your good deeds glow for all to see, so that
they will praise your heavenly Father.*
MATTHEW 5:16 TLB

God shines bright through hearts trusting
fully and fearlessly. Don't ever think you're
not good enough, changed enough, or gifted
enough—just trust and *shine your light*. You have
one. It came with your first breath, complete
with God's radiance. There's no measure for
a good deed; if it's done in love, it's infinitely
good, and it's going to point a hurting heart to
a heavenly Father.

Father, show the world Your light through me.

I will tell everyone how good You are,
and of Your constant, daily care.
PSALM 71:15 TLB

Let's go with the little things to tell the world
how good God is: a hug…a "How can I help
you?"…a smile…a moment of eye contact to
really listen…a few words with some hope in
them. They're such clear reflectors of the
God who has us in His constant, daily care.
Day-to-day kindnesses feel like love notes
from God when we get them, and we should
be even better at giving them.

He will keep in perfect peace all those who trust
in Him, whose thoughts turn often to the Lord!
ISAIAH 26:3 TLB

The thought of God keeping us in perfect peace if we think about Him often sounds like a pretty perfect exchange. Days are rarely without bumps, stresses, and challenges, so to know we're a thought—a *moment*—away from the quiet, calming presence of God is enough to face the day with courage. Trust is letting go of our cares to let God care for *everything*—and that is a powerful, peace-filled promise.

Lord, let my thoughts turn to You today when
my heart is in need of Your perfect peace.

It is good for me to draw near to God;
I have put my trust in the GOD.
PSALM 73:28 NKJV

No turning our backs today, Lord, just trust
and hope in You. We know You're right
here, closer than our next breath, not going
anywhere. We choose to face Your love full
on. Our hearts need the rest and comfort,
our souls the hope and peace. We'll just be
still today, inside, even though the world
around us is loud and busy. There's solace
in knowing that You're never too busy for us
because we're infinitely valuable to You.

Lord, I'll spend my day near to You
and trust Your perfect love for me.

*...My grace is sufficient for you, for My
strength is made perfect in weakness....*
II CORINTHIANS 12:9 NKJV

Mistakes like to be loud and persistent.
They bully truth and grace with shame. But
weaknesses are fertile ground for humility and
humanness. If we never stand in the muddy
messiness of our shortcomings, we might forget
to wash our souls in grace, the astounding favor
that is ours just because God loves us. And that's
right where His strength is...in the place where
we understand how helpless and human we are
without Him.

*Father, thank You for favor and forgiveness and
the strength that meets me in my weakness.*

I walk in the strength of GOD.
PSALM 71:16 TLB

It's time to open it, the gift of another day.
Feeling out of sorts, discouraged, tired?
Unwrap it anyway; you're going to find just
what you need—because it's just what God put
in it: love bigger than any disappointment,
grace so amazing it'll pick up the pieces
of your heart and hold you, comforting…
forgiving. Strength? Hope? It's all here in
Him. And He's rooting for brave you.

Lord, thank You for being everything I need today.

The LORD directs the steps of the godly. He
delights in every detail of their lives.
PSALM 37:23 NLT

Our days. All these moments put together,
and we hope we get more of them right than
wrong. How is it that God delights in the
details of our lives even if we're not getting
all the moments right? Because His love for
us doesn't change when our hearts get out of
step with His. He keeps right on directing us
toward His purpose—and He knows it's going
to be good.

Lord, keep me on the path of Your purpose
and help me to stay in step with Your love.

Trust in the LORD and do good.
PSALM 37:3 NLT

The truth about giving kindness and goodness is that it's really about "getting" it—that life is hard at times and sometimes we forget that it's not about us. We live it, but we can't give it, and being kind and good and loving are the best ways to point hearts to the One who can.

Father, let my actions today lead others to You.

He holds our lives in His hands, and
He holds our feet to the path.
PSALM 66:9 TLB

Andrew Murray wrote, "I am in God's charge. My God is working out my life for me." So this is the bottom line today, to open your eyes and get ready to see God work, to look for moments to love on someone, to surrender to His lead. Steps are planned and He's holding you steady, so if things don't go according to paper lists and mental to-dos, just smile through—God is guiding you.

Lord, my feet are steady on the path of
Your plan. I rest in trusting You.

I am the First and the Last; there is no other God.
ISAIAH 44:6 TLB

Whatever today holds, know God is holding you. From the first waking moment to the crawling or falling into bed, He's got you in His hands because He loves you with all His heart. It might not go perfectly and patience might run out and faith is going to be tested. But God is close with the grace you need—and He'll be strong when you can't.

Father, from beginning to end, Your grace and love are the strength of my heart today.

God is working in you, giving you the desire
and the power to do what pleases Him.
PHILIPPIANS 2:13 NLT

You have God's full attention today. His love has no boundaries, no end, no limits. It's at work in you for the special things He has planned for you to do. He's changed your heart already, and every day He's getting you ready for greater things. His preparation gives you power—to be all you can be, love all you can reach, and trust all things to Him.

Father, thank You for loving me and
preparing me to be Your love to others.

...Your right hand has held me up, Your
gentleness has made me great. You enlarged
my path under me, so my feet did not slip.
PSALM 18:35—36 NKJV

The gentleness of the most gentle, most
loving, most merciful greets your day with
a promise that He's put you on the way to
great things. You don't have to worry about
how you'll hold up through the storms;
you're being held up by the One who chases
them with peace, hope, joy, and a love that
never lets up. Trust that you're on the path
of divine purposes and know every step is
guided with grace.

Father, I trust You with the steps I take and the
choices I make, knowing Your love leads me.

He fills me with strength and protects me wherever I go.
PSALM 18:32 TLB

When it's hard to get up and not give up, there's strength standing ready to give you what you need—and remind your heart why God needs you. There are lives in the world you're made to love by reflecting the love that made you. And with His love comes protection, powered by a perfect Savior. You can't be replaced—and you won't find a place more empowering than His love.

Lord, Your strength is my shield,
Your love my purpose.

*...Every path He guides us on is fragrant
with His loving-kindness and His truth.*
PSALM 25:10 TLB

The God-guided path is kind, loving, and
good. It's good for making our hearts more
like His, our eyes wide open to see the needs
of others, and our arms more willing to help
the hurting. We're the sweet fragrance of
Christ and the truth bearers of hope and the
signposts of grace. Our days are opportunities
to stay aware on the path we travel—and bring
glory to the One who guides us.

*Father, make my heart more like Yours today,
guiding me on the path that glorifies You.*

...Give yourselves completely to God—every part of you...to be used for His good purposes.
ROMANS 6:13 TLB

Every part of you holds heavenly purposes. The hands that stitched you together made it so, so you can be sure that even the broken pieces pushed deep down, out of sight, out of use...*never are.* God makes the most beautiful work of shattered souls, with healing that holds strong and love that lights them brighter still, drawing the lives of the hurt, the helpless, and the heartbroken to the hope of Him.

Father, take what is broken in me and make it useful for the healing of others.

*…You know me inside and out…You
know exactly how I was made…*
PSALM 139:15 THE MESSAGE

To be known is such a sweet way to be loved.
God knows you, and, wow, does He love
you—like no one on earth ever will and more
than anything in the universe that can be
measured. And it isn't just our grace-washed,
love-rebuilt inside—God loves our dust-
particle, time-sensitive outside too—our
humanness that needs Him daily to forgive and
fix and strengthen. Lean hard into His all-
consuming love today, knowing it knows your
every need.

*Lord, Your love for me is boundless, meeting me
where I'm at today and meeting every need.*

...Whatever I have, wherever I am, I can make it through anything in the One who makes me who I am.
PHILIPPIANS 4:13 THE MESSAGE

Soul contentment never comes from *what* we have; it comes from *Who* we have, because He makes us who we *are*. Only God can fill the real needs: love, forgiveness, strength, hope, joy, purpose. Never stop hoping for what you want while being content with where you are now. Everything can change, and often does, in a moment of a day that looks ordinary—because our days belong to an extraordinary God.

Father, I'm content with the place
I'm in, because You are my all.

Now faith is the substance of things hoped
for, the evidence of things not seen.
HEBREWS 11:1 NKJV

We have them. Days when faith feels faint and
we feel have failed. Tears well up to roll down
our fighting-to-smile faces because we can't
squeeze an ounce of hope to the altar through
the ache. We want to *see* what we've hoped for
and *touch* what we've prayed for. Then we press
in and God *is*—the next breath, the last tear
wiped away. And He is at work. In you...for
you...to amaze you.

Father, I trust You with every hope in the midst
of every tear and know You are right here.

Work with enthusiasm, as though you were
working for the Lord rather than for people.
EPHESIANS 6:7 NLT

Let our hands reach into the lives of others
with God's love and nothing more. No
expectations or judgments, no agendas
or questions. Just a continuous stream of
heaven's love seeping from our smile and
our words and the things we do. There isn't
anything more important today. Love is
all and it's what we all need. It guides every
heart to a glorious Savior and does nothing
but good.

Lord, I give all that I am to giving all love
today. Thank You for showing me the way.

...His favor lasts a lifetime!

PSALM 30:5 NLT

All this favor poured over your life from the God who loves you...let it overflow. His presence and delight in you...let it run from your fingertips into acts of kindness, hope-heavy words, and little deeds done with big love. Stay awake to the needs around you and the power within you. It can make all the difference today.

Father, let Your presence and love move my heart to act for the good of others today.

This is the day the Lord has made. We
will rejoice and be glad in it.
PSALM 118:24 TLB

Today is already written by God's hand.
Let's let Him lead. Our human obligations
will never outweigh the divine order of our
moments. He's in control. And that's where
we find the peace that gets pushed out by the
stress. So when it feels like things are spinning
wild and plans are changing and nerves are
fraying, remember Who saw it all, steers it all,
and uses it all to grow our trust in Him.

Lord, give me peace in the moments today,
knowing they're all penned by Your hand.

...Be happy. Grow in Christ... Live
in harmony and peace....
II CORINTHIANS 13:11

Here we are with another day to grow. I hope we cultivate the good stuff—the *God* stuff. Love that helps eyes see what Jesus is like and life-giving words that help a heart feel unforgotten and a little less lonely. And I hope we live happy and thankful, knowing the moments are for making better moments for those around us.

Father, help me grow into more of
Your likeness and love today.

*Let's not get tired of doing what is good. At
just the right time we will reap a harvest
of blessing if we don't give up.*
GALATIANS 6:9 NLT

For the tired, the torn, and the tried in the
world around us, let's not get tired of doing
what's good—of *being* good for the One who is
the greatest good. Grace is our go-to energy
source to overcome a life-wearied heart. God
will never give up on us. Let's give today's
moments and fill them with good.

*Father, fuel my heart with Your grace today,
so I can do what's good for Your glory.*

*I will praise You, for I am fearfully and
wonderfully made; marvelous are Your works,
and that my soul knows very well.*
PSALM 139:14 NKJV

God's works are *always* marvelous. And you're
one of them. Spend some moments today
thanking Him for the gift of your life and
the miracle of who you are. You're filled with
wonder and His wonderful purposes. God's
love created every fiber of your being for every
plan He has for you—and they're carried out
with His love because He carries you in the
palm of His hand.

*Father, thank You for the miracle of life and
the love in all that You've planned for me.*

God is able to make all grace abound toward you,
that you, always having all sufficiency in all things,
may have an abundance for every good work.
II CORINTHIANS 9:8 NKJV

Hard days strengthen and teach us that God
is good no matter what and grace stands
sufficient. There's simply no giving up in the
face of grace. It's too much proof of God's
love and too humbling to ignore—and it
never gives up on us. God knows that when
our hearts grow stronger He can grow the
scope of His purpose in us, and He wants
nothing more than to increase our view.

Father, give me the strength of Your grace and
love and help me trust You completely.

Be full of love for others, following
the example of Christ...
EPHESIANS 5:2 TLB

He's incredibly full of love for us, our Savior. Spilled on the cross, His love became salvation for every seeking soul. And what the seeking souls need to see in us is Him, the Holy One who makes them whole—with love that's perfect and personal, unconditional and unending, full and forgiving. Let that be our longing today: emulate His example.

Lord, fill me with Your love so the world
can see that my heart is full of You.

…Let's not just talk about love; let's practice real love.
1 JOHN 3:18 THE MESSAGE

There's the leftover to-do list from yesterday and the new day pressing in and waiting for answers to prayers whispered from a weary heart at night…and one more thing to think about sounds like one thing too much. But if we pare down what needs to be practiced today, it's the one and only thing that truly matters. *Love.* And real love isn't work; it's worship.

Lord, I want to put Your love into practice today through my actions. Help my heart be sensitive to the needs of others.

...Fear not, for I am with you and will bless you....
GENESIS 26:24 TLB

Be fearless today. Absolutely nothing is going to stop God's plan for you or stall His purposes in you. You might think you have to accomplish more, that the routine of your days can't be part of the *real* plan. But God can make anything happen from anywhere, anytime that He chooses. And since *you're* chosen, believe you're right where you belong—and be the brightest reflection of Him you can be.

Father, I will follow You fearlessly,
knowing You're working out Your plan
with perfect love and timing.

Commit everything you do to the Lord. Trust
Him to help you do it, and He will.
PSALM 37:5 TLB

Everything done today will be with excellence
and for His glory. Not only does God honor
that attitude, but He helps us deliver it.
It's not truly beautiful and best if it's not
done with love. Whatever the day holds, be
confident that He's holding *you* and dive in.
Trust in His help, mirror His heart, and be
the light of His love.

Lord, I commit the work of my hands to You,
today, in the excellence of Your love.

...We confidently and joyfully look forward to actually
becoming all that God has had in mind for us to be.
ROMANS 5:2 TLB

We're being shaped by God's hand for His
purposes. Today is part of the sculpting. Even
when we feel there's more we should or could
be doing, trusting God to do His work in us
means believing that days are never wasted.
He isn't idle. When we focus on what's in
front of us, we allow God to use the *now* things
to move us to the *next* thing.

Father, help me see and appreciate the ways I'm
becoming all that You have in mind for me to be.

Love us, God, with all You've got—
that's what we're depending on.
PSALM 33:22 THE MESSAGE

Sometimes the faith we're able to pull from our world-weary souls is just enough to get us through the day, and sometimes, only a few of the hard moments. *That's okay.* Even when our faith is thin and we're in the thick of a tough season, God's loving us with all He's got—and He promises...*He's got us* no matter what.

Father, Your love is my constant comfort.
I depend on You to carry me through.

*And yet, O Lord, You are our Father. We are the clay
and You are the Potter. We are all formed by Your hand.*
ISAIAH 64:8 TLB

Resting in God's hand, we're formed into
fullness. He created us and now He completes
us. Our hearts are learning to love others,
our eyes are opening to see the needs, our
hands are becoming more willing to serve.
God *gives*...and He gives us moments in every
single day to be a vessel He can use to fill
some small space with larger-than-life love.

*Lord, I surrender to the sculpting of Your hand
today. Let me be a vessel filled with love.*

...We can be mirrors that brightly
reflect the glory of the Lord...
II CORINTHIANS 3:18 TLB

Let the world see God in the mirror of your life today. Let others feel the light of His love streaming from you. Let them feel the warmth of His presence when you're present as you spread some joy with a simple smile. Life gets heavy sometimes, but there's One who can lift the care from shoulders, the confusion from minds, and the hurt from hearts—and it's a blessing to let Him do it through you.

Lord, let me reflect all that You are
to all the lives I touch today.

*...And as the Spirit of the Lord works within
us, we become more and more like Him.*
II CORINTHIANS 3:18 TLB

What if we didn't carry a care today? What if
we decided right this moment to give them
all to the One calling us closer? What if we
snuggled in and learned to be more like Him:
slow to get angry...quick to forgive...filled
with love...emptied of self? It's astounding to
think He won't give up on us, no matter how
many messes we make with our wild, unruly
hearts. But He won't—because He knows love
will win.

*Lord, Your Spirit transforms my heart
daily by the power of Your love.
Thank You for never giving up on me.*

...Cultivate God-confidence.
I CORINTHIANS 10:12 THE MESSAGE

Believe with all your heart that God is all you need. Stand in the midst of the storm and live your day surrendered to His lead. Doubt is a weapon of discouragement. It steals the confidence God wants you to have in the promise that He will never leave or fail you. You belong to Him and your battles belong in His hand, because He knows that wins become worship and trust turns into triumph.

Father, fill me with the confidence of
Your unfailing promises today.

*For You are great, and do wondrous
things; You alone are God.*
PSALM 86:10 NKJV

Sometimes the wait can weigh us down. Long
days of hope and hanging on make our hearts
heavy, and we wonder, *Where are the wondrous
things?* They're coming. They're being worked
out by the God of miracles to bring the best
possible outcome in our lives. In the heaviness
remember the holiness of everything given
to us through His heart—because it's always
enveloped in love.

*Father, give me the strength to stay secure in
hope. Your love is working out what's best.*

MAY 2

…Throw yourselves into the work of the
Master, confident that nothing you do for
Him is a waste of time or effort.
I CORINTHIANS 15:58 THE MESSAGE

If we start our day with the mind-set that
everything we do matters, everything we do
will make a difference. Life is made up of
ordinary moments only God sees. These
are extraordinary opportunities to worship,
to listen, to be still, and to get our hearts
saturated with love before pouring into the
hundreds of daily things to come. The work
of the Master is always about love. Let the
things you do point the world to Him.

Father, I know that all I do for You matters.
Bless the work of my hands with Your love.

Let the peace of God rule in your
hearts...and be thankful.
COLOSSIANS 3:15 NKJV

The heart-rule for today is peace. Be at peace knowing that you're chosen and God is in all you do today in a big way. There are no small plans for you—not if you belong to Him. Your hands are touching eternity all while you're patient when you feel frustrated... loving when you feel spent...thankful when you feel worn out. He sees that courageous heart in you...and that makes Him thankful for *you*.

Lord, give me Your perfect peace, and let me
serve You with a thankful heart today.

*...Let your light shine.... For the glory
of the Lord is streaming from you.*
ISAIAH 60:1 TLB

Shine the love of God on your corner of the
world, toward the faces that are in front of
you daily, on that holy ground called home.
The challenge to love is maybe a little more
real here at times, in the comfort of raw
emotions and our real selves. Be kind here
first. Always. And trust God to strengthen
the love inside the four walls so there will be
plenty of courage to love outside them.

*Father, I pray for a home where Your
love shines brightly from every heart.*

Following after the Holy Spirit leads to life and peace...
ROMANS 8:6 TLB

There's a chance not everything will go the way we plan for the day. But it *will* go as God planned. When nerves start to unravel, remember to take a moment to check with God on the change of direction. *Am I supposed to take a minute to listen? Is this detour protecting me? Should I pick up this call?* Don't confuse distractions with divine order. Keep your heart peaceful and let His plan prevail.

Father, fill my heart with peace as
I follow Your plan today.

...Our only power and success comes from God.
II CORINTHIANS 3:5 TLB

Success is getting love down to an art—to paint the world with strokes of kindness and gentleness and generosity, to put a spotlight on God's grace. Love has the power to change lives; we have the privilege of sharing it. Not for a moment can we take credit for the love we have to give; it's all Him. And it always creates something beautiful.

Father, let every life I touch today see
the beauty of Your love in me.

...We never give up...our inner strength
in the Lord is growing every day.
II CORINTHIANS 4:16 TLB

It's going be harder some days, this grace
walk. We won't feel deserving and maybe
we won't see a way through. But God sees
you on the other side of the difficult days
and the discouragement, *because He's carrying*
you there—and when He puts your feet back
on the ground, see how you've grown even
stronger still.

Lord, I won't give up on Your faithfulness to me,
knowing Your strength is my heart's reward.

*May my spoken words and unspoken
thoughts be pleasing even to You,
O Lord my Rock and my Redeemer.*
PSALM 19:14 TLB

The words we choose today—let them be spirit-lifting and smile-bringing. Let them give courage, inspire joy, and show understanding. Let them be kind, filled with love, and filtered by grace. And let the choices begin with our thoughts, by keeping them positive and praiseworthy. God spoke words and the earth came to be—*that's* how much weight they carry and how life-giving they can be.

*Lord, give me the wisdom to choose the right
words and to always respond with love.*

You are my hiding place from every storm of life...
PSALM 32:7 TLB

We've all had them, days when the burdens bearing down make it hard to get up and start the day. The covers over our eyes feel right in moments that ache deep, ..untouched by words. Our hearts find a faint prayer: *Where do we go from here?* We go to the One who knew we'd need a hiding place, so He became one. Away from the world and the worries, God holds us tight, all the way back to hope again, comforting until the storm calms. No matter how difficult the day, God is with us to make a way.

Father, You're my refuge in the storm
and my hope until the sun shines again.

…Abiding love surrounds those who trust in the Lord.
PSALM 32:10 TLB

It's a great day to trust God with everything you've got—and everything you've got going. Maybe there are a few things you're not looking forward to, maybe there's some stuff you're not sure of, maybe there's a care you haven't quite let go of. There's a love surrounding you that's not going anywhere, and it's not giving up on you. It's full of courage and hope and strength—anything you need—and it's coming from the One who put a purpose in you nothing can stop.

Lord, I trust You to give the strength I need for every step toward Your purposes.

*I will instruct you (says the Lord) and guide
you along the best pathway for your life...*
PSALM 32:8 TLB

There's a good pathway for our life, and then
there's the *best* one. What's best for us takes
listening to Him and getting out of the way to
let God have His way. We like to hang on to
a little control; it's humanness and fear that
don't let God have it all. But He's guiding us
with an instruction manual written before
we were born. Rewriting pages will only add
steps on the way to His best.

Father, I surrender to You on the way to Your best.

As far as God is concerned there is a sweet,
wholesome fragrance in our lives. It is
the fragrance of Christ within us...
II CORINTHIANS 2:15 TLB

A servant heart draws a searching one. Be the kindness today, the love that goes out of its way, the smile, the hope, the compassion. Everyone is going through life and getting knocked down. Lift. Light. Listen. Be to others what God is to you—and help a fellow traveler find their way through.

Father, let me be the sweet fragrance
of Christ in the world today.

For God has said, "I will never, never
fail you or forsake you."
HEBREWS 13:5 TLB

What you go through in life, you will never go through alone. From the tears that fall in the quiet hours to the sadness you feel closing in at times, God sees it all—and He's moving things into place that you can't see now but will. You'll see your hopes come to life, you'll see your desires unfold, and you'll see God's love for you in a way you've never seen before.

Father, You fill my life with Your unfailing
love. All my trust and hope is in You.

No matter what happens, always be thankful, for this is God's will for you who belong to Christ Jesus.
I THESSALONIANS 5:18 TLB

How can all these tough things be the *right* things when God is so good? The truth is, we'd never comprehend the fathomless goodness without the soul-piercing suffering. And our suffering will never compare to the One who prays for us day and night with pierced hands. God's will is for us to be willing...to thank Him, to trust Him, and to love Him no matter what.

Father, thank You for giving me hope in all things at all times. I'm trusting You.

...Let love guide your life...
COLOSSIANS 3:14 TLB

It's the one thing we can't take off the to-do list today: love. It should be our guide, our guiding force and what we look forward to getting better at every time our feet hit the floor in the morning. What we do in life doesn't matter much if love isn't in it, because God is love and He matters most.

Father, fuel me with love today so the world will see and seek You.

MAY 16

…When troubles of any kind come your way,
consider it an opportunity for great joy. For
you know that when your faith is tested,
your endurance has a chance to grow.

JAMES 1:2–3 NLT

Be thankful for the work God's doing in you even when it's difficult. Choose joy on days that aren't easy. Hold on to your faith with both hands and know that your heart is growing stronger. Every moment of your life is sifted through God's love and what's going to open your eyes to more of it.

Lord, thank You for loving me and growing
my faith in You for greater things.

After you have suffered a little while, our God,
who is full of kindness through Christ, will
give you His eternal glory. He personally will
come and pick you up, and set you firmly in
place, and make you stronger than ever.

I PETER 5:10 TLB

Some days we just need a little pick-me-up.
Other days we need God to step in and pick us
up with the all-consuming love He's made of
and give us the strength to stand. If that's what
you need today, you have it. Lean in. Let Him
be close. Let Him have everything. Let Him
keep you going when you think you can't. And
when the battle's won, look at you—stronger
than ever.

Father, I'll rest in the cradle of Your arms
today and let You be my strength.

...My purpose is to give life in all its fullness.
JOHN 10:10 TLB

Every path has purpose. Even the ones with pitfalls and pity parties we throw in solitude when our minds fill up with *why* and *how much longer*? If we want God's fullness, we have to trust Him fully. And what He sees that we can't is the moment our hearts are ready for the great things He has planned for us.

Lord, thank You for the fullness
of Your life and grace.

Instantly Jesus reached out his hand and
rescued him. "O man of little faith," Jesus
said. "Why did you doubt me?"
MATTHEW 14:31 TLB

There are no day passes for doubt. It can't
have a place in us when our hope is placed
firmly in God. Once we've prayed about
the job, the child, the needs, the dream, we
have to let go and let the cries of our heart
make their way to the heart of God. And the
moment you're heard, love answers—and it
will come to you at the perfect time, with the
most compassion.

Lord, I put my hope in You and my doubts to rest.

*For whatever is born of God overcomes
the world. And this is the victory that has
overcome the world—our faith.*
I JOHN 5:4 NKJV

Throw yourself into the day, heart ready. Ready
to overcome discouragement with hope, disappointments with joy, and difficulties with
strength. God's got everything you need
with sufficiency that never wanes. And all we
need is faith the size of a seed to move any
mountain in the way of our blessed-beyond-
measure day.

*Father, make my heart ready for all the
good things You've put in my day.*

*Let every detail in your lives—words, actions,
whatever—be done in the name of the Master, Jesus,
thanking God the Father every step of the way.*
COLOSSIANS 3:17 THE MESSAGE

The words we choose today are an act
of worship. The way we respond to the
unexpected should bring honor to His name.
Every detail, from the morning bustle to
the evening wind-down, should reflect our
love for Jesus. Serving Him in the mundane
moments is no less important than standing
in the spotlight with the world watching. It's
all for our growth and His glory.

Father, let everything I do reflect and honor You.

*...He surrounds me with loving-kindness and
tender mercies. He fills my life with good things...*
PSALM 103:4–5 TLB

Peace will come, joy will surface, hope will
emerge, and our hearts will rest when we
give God control and focus on Him. Don't
we want His infinite goodness? Yes, we do,
but sometimes we go our own way and bury
our wounded and wayward hearts in worldly
things. But He stands at the ready for our
undivided attention, responding to it with
His immeasurable grace.

*Father, thank You for the promise
of Your love and mercy.*

You have hedged me behind and before,
and laid Your hand upon me.
PSALM 139:5 NKJV

Being encompassed by God means being set gloriously free. Free from the struggle of feeling inferior, unloved, underappreciated. Free from wondering how things will turn out or if needs will be met this month. Not only does His presence surround us, but His hand of blessing is on us too. So, today, let's be free and fully charged with faith. God is fighting for us on all sides.

Father, I'm at peace because You are here.

Fill the followers of God with joy...
PSALM 70:4 TLB

Joy isn't always how we feel; it's always how we're *strong*. We have to have God in the heart to keep joy in our days. His stuff is the real stuff. When we believe everything is going to work out and worries can be washed away by grace, we get happy. Truly happy.

Lord, I'm going to give all my cares to You and carry Your joy into my day.

*Whatever is good and perfect is a gift coming
down to us from God the Father, who created all
the lights in the heavens. He never changes...*
JAMES 1:17 NLT

All the lights in the heavens were called into
place by the same One who created you. The
One who has so much love for You that He'd
do anything for you—so He decided to give
everything He had. There's no lack in His gift
of grace. It's all you need to live a life so full
of what your heart craves that there's no need
left to fill—and there never will be.

*Father, Your love for me will never change.
Thank You for every good gift You've given.*

*...Trust your lives to the God who created
you, for He will never fail you.*
I PETER 4:19 NLT

Trust that God is right here, right now. You
are never alone. You are never ignored. God
is paying close attention to everything that
concerns you...the sad, the happy, and every
moment in between. Today there will be
glimpses of His love sent just for you. Look
for every one of them and let them make your
heart feel loved.

Lord, Your presence is my peace today.

*Be gracious in your speech. The goal is to
bring out the best in others in a conversation,
not put them down, not cut them out.*
COLOSSIANS 4:6 THE MESSAGE

Using words to bring out the best in others takes letting God bring out the best in us. How does He speak to us? "You are precious to me and honored, and I love you" (Isaiah 43:4 TLB). It doesn't get any more gracious than that. If we put a "grace guard" on our conversations, there would be a lot more smiles in the world...and a lot of hearts feeling loved.

*Lord, let the words I speak today
be seasoned with Your love.*

*…God who began the good work within you will
keep right on helping you grow in His grace…*
PHILIPPIANS 1:6 TLB

God will never quit on you. He chose you,
He changed you, and He cherishes you. Every
time you face a challenge to your faith, He
uses it to show You how high and wide and
wonderful His grace is. You can't exhaust it.
You won't reach the end of it. And His good
work in you will go on.

*Father, thank You for grace and the
work You're doing within me.*

...The Lord your God will bless you...
in all the work of your hands...
DEUTERONOMY 16:15 NKJV

The moments when we're mindful of God will always make a difference. When it doesn't seem like the ordinary course of our day is ordered by God, we have to believe with all our hearts that it is. When we start to feel that the path God paves must be more elaborate, we need to recall the steps of our Savior—personal interactions, sharing meals, telling stories. Simple things can often make the most significant, and eternal, impressions.

Lord, I know that all things You will for my life matter. Help me see the gift in each one.

MAY 30

Devote yourselves to prayer with an
alert mind and a thankful heart.
COLOSSIANS 4:2 NLT

Let's keep our hearts praying today. Even if the words don't make a sound, God hears us. He's here, in the silent places that harbor anxiety and pain and worries. And it's a comfort to have a constant listener. More than that, One who answers…with love, peace, strength, and a few words of His own: *I will never leave you.*

Father, thank You for hearing all my heart is
saying today and for answering with all grace.

*Don't be selfish; don't live to make a good
impression on others. Be humble, thinking
of others as better than yourselves.*
PHILIPPIANS 2:3 TLB

Put people first. Look for ways to bless
others. It can be as simple as letting someone
go in front of you at the grocery store or a
smile just because it's the nice thing and the
right thing to do. We're all in this together,
seeing the same sad news and gut-wrenching
headlines. That's why glimpses of God in the
smallest action can be the biggest way to share
His love.

*Lord, open my eyes and my heart to
ways I can show Your love today.*

JUNE 1

For with God nothing will be impossible.
LUKE 1:37 NKJV

You have a new day in front of you, full of possibility—with God, maybe an *impossibility* too. Miracles happen in moments. Press on and keep believing if you're believing for something only He can make happen. When it gets here, your faith will start a wildfire in you that spreads like crazy because the world is going to see the truth burning: God keeps His promises—and promises His best.

Father, hopes and dreams are in Your hand. I put my faith and hope in You.

*Oh, how grateful and thankful I am to
the Lord because He is so good...*
PSALM 7:17 TLB

God is good all the time. We've heard it a
million times, and as life goes on, we believe
it a million times more. He's *always* good. Even
when circumstances aren't and the news we
get isn't. He's still good. Even when days are
long and our patience is short and everything
goes wrong and we don't think it's right. God
is good and here's a great truth: He's working
everything together for our good.

*Lord, You're always good, and I trust the
good You're working together in my life.*

I am holding you by your right hand....
Don't be afraid; I am here to help you.
ISAIAH 41:13 TLB

Do you need a hand today? The God who
counts the stars and counts every life priceless
is holding your hand, so fear has to go. You
have all the help you'll need to walk smoothly
through the rough patches and stand tall
in the face of things that bring your heart
down. You can live the moments happily...
hopefully...and full to the top with love. Have
that kind of day—you have God holding you.

Father, in Your heart I'm priceless.
Thank You for holding on to me.

The Lord is close to those whose hearts are breaking.
PSALM 34:18 TLB

You can feel Him there, when your heart is crushed to powder and the winds of hopelessness carry every tiny fragment away. Who's going to put this back together? Who can pick up every piece—*find* every piece? Only One. And He *will*. God is close to broken hearts because He's the healer of them, the builder who puts them back together, because He loves us more than our broken, rebuilt hearts will ever, ever fathom.

Father, thank You for being close and loving
me back together when I'm broken.

Be strong! Be courageous!…
For the Lord your God will be with you…
DEUTERONOMY 31:6 TLB

You are loved, appreciated, brave, and one-of-a-kind. This is a God-designed day, written for you. It might call on the courage He's grown in you through challenges or the strength that's come through brokenness and a thousand tears. He holds you up for others to see because you held Him while the battle raged. Be a light today—you're shining brighter than ever before.

Lord, use me to be a light in the lives of others today.

My God is changeless in His love for me...
PSALM 59:10 TLB

You're loved in this moment, just the way you are, and you're on your way to becoming all God created you to be. We're works in progress. Every day is a fight against the flesh and the doing-it-our-way because, truthfully, it's easier. It's even easier to believe that there's no way God can love us in our mess. But He does...and especially there, where our need for Him is glaring.

Father, Your love for me is incredible
and unconditional. I rest in the
promise that it never changes.

Lead me by Your truth and teach me, for You are the God who saves me. All day long I put my hope in You.
PSALM 25:5 NLT

Every day is a fresh start and a new opportunity to let the past go and let God lead. All day long and especially on the long days there's nothing more healing than hoping in Him. He leads with love that doesn't stop when we slip, strength that doesn't slip when we struggle, and the Holy Spirit, who never struggles to stay right with us through it all.

Lord, You are my hope and the One who leads me with the mightiest love I know.

May the Lord lead your hearts into a full
understanding and expression of the love of God and
the patient endurance that comes from Christ.
II THESSALONIANS 3:5 NLT

Our hearts are learning today, and there's so, so much. The fullness of the love that saved us and continues to save us in every battle—that's a start. Then there's long-suffering, tested daily at some point—sometimes when we're impatient and unforgiving with ourselves. Jesus suffered long and endured all for the amazing grace we're given a lifetime to understand. And it won't be long enough to discover a fraction of its depth.

Lord, teach my heart to be like Yours.

...Now we have confidence in a better hope,
through which we draw near to God.
HEBREWS 7:19 NLT

The right path will always draw our hearts closer to God. Hope will be a signpost— because if our hope is in anything or anyone other than Him, it's a waste of our time. Hope in God will put confidence in our souls to go the right way for all the right reasons.

Father, I put my confidence and
my hope in You alone.

When the Holy Spirit controls our lives he will
produce this kind of fruit in us: love, joy, peace,
patience, kindness, goodness, faithfulness...
GALATIANS 5:22 TLB

If we list our goals for every day, the Spirit-
led fruit list should always be on it. But,
alas, we remember how human we are when
patience runs thin and unkind words jump
out and hearts get bruised a little...even our
own. That's the moment we stand back up,
take the basket from the Holy Spirit, and put
our broken-but-forgiven hearts into picking
up the fruit we dropped. And by grace alone,
we begin again.

Father, give me the strength to produce—and
share—the fruit of Your Spirit today.

I want you woven into a tapestry of love, in touch with everything there is to know of God. Then you will have minds confident and at rest, focused on Christ...
COLOSSIANS 2:2 THE MESSAGE

Our hearts are peaceful when our focus is God. If our minds are on any other thing for more of the time than we're mindful of Him, we lose our spiritual balance. It doesn't feel good to be off-balance, and it's hard for us to do good when we are. If we keep our focus on Jesus, our lives, and the lives of those around us, fill up with love—and nothing feels better than that.

Father, my focus is on You today and my heart is at peace in Your love.

When you draw close to God, God
will draw close to you...
JAMES 4:8 TLB

Today, let's get closer to the One who is love
and draw from His power. His strength will
make us strong to face trials, our fearless
steps as sure as His promise of victory. His
compassion will make us tender enough to
see the needs we might have missed with our
finite, human eyes. His forgiveness will make
us forgiving of the faults of others and help
us see the need in ourselves. Let's make the
life journey easier for others today by getting
closer to the Life-giver in us.

Father, I'm drawing closer to You today and
asking for a heart that is more like Yours.

*Who are those who fear the Lord? He will
show them the path they should choose.*
PSALM 25:12 NLT

Every choice we make and every path we take
should be decided through prayer and peace.
God will lead us—and His answers will have
the best, most loving effect on the greatest
number of people. Love is never selfish, and
God leads us with love. If there is a decision
to make today, ask God…and wait for peace.

*Father, lead me with Your love and peace today
and give me the wisdom to choose Your way.*

*...You must learn to know God better and
discover what He wants you to do.*
II PETER 1:5 TLB

Knowing God better makes *us* better. Better
at serving and loving, better to our families,
better friends, better at whatever we're doing
every day. There's no class system for good
souls—they learn to be good and do good if
they accept grace, look to the cross, and learn
to love God. It is *first* and *always* about love.

*Father, I want to learn to know You better so
that I can love You, and others, even more.*

*...We can all be saved in this same way,
by coming to Christ, no matter who we
are or what we have been like.*
ROMANS 3:22 TLB

It wasn't pretty, my heart. Before coming to Jesus there was too much of me. God does create us wonderfully and marvelously, but He's the beautiful part of who we are. We can't make it through this earth journey without His grace and love. They transform us and form us into the likeness of Him whom the world needs—and He needs the new you in your part of the world today.

*Lord, I surrender to Your transforming,
redeeming grace today. Let my life reflect You.*

God arms me with strength, and
he makes my way perfect.
PSALM 18:32 NLT

Strength for anything coming at you today—
that's what God has given you. If you need
to call on that strength to get through some
difficult moments, remember that He's also
made your way perfect. It might not always
look like perfection to us, but we don't want
our way; we want His—because that's the way
our souls will become more beautiful.

Father, give me the strength to
follow Your perfect way.

JUNE 17

*It is God Himself who has made us what we are
and given us new lives from Christ Jesus...*
EPHESIANS 2:10 TLB

We're not our true selves until we're fully
surrendered to Christ. We need the renewed
us to give everything to the One who made
the way for us to become new. We find our
unique and wonderful selves there, in the
midst of the love that created us. It's the very
best we will *ever* be when we make it our prayer
to be like Him.

*Lord, Your life is the most beautiful part of who
I am. Give me more of who You are today.*

...The real life I now have...is a result of my trusting in the Son of God, who loved me and gave Himself for me.
GALATIANS 2:20 TLB

It's a sweet trust that leads our hearts to the cross. Standing there, we face a love so unbelievable and hard to comprehend that it shakes us to our core. But that's right where Jesus wants to be—in the deepest part of our hearts, depositing the greatest truths of God's grace.

Father, Your life is the real life in me, Your grace and love my reason for living.

I walk in the strength of the Lord God...
You alone are just and good.
PSALM 71:16 TLB

God makes good things happen. Our days are filled with the hopes of what we want to do and people in our lives we want to bless. We want God's best for our home and everyone in it. When we walk in the strength God gives, we strengthen our hold on faith—and in His perfect time, our faith will become sight.

Father, You are the keeper and the giver of all
that I hope for. I put my faith in You alone.

For Jehovah God is our Light and our Protector.
He gives us grace and glory. No good thing will he
withhold from those who walk along His paths.
PSALM 84:11 TLB

You're on the path God has chosen. You'll
know He's brought you to the place you are
now because when you look back, you'll see
His *why* in every step you've taken. You'll
see the footprints of His grace and the light
of His glory. He's guiding you today too...
and you're on the way to some incredibly
good things.

Father, thank You for guiding my steps by Your
grace into every good thing You have for my life.

JUNE 21

*After the earthquake, there was a fire, but
the Lord was not in the fire...after the fire,
there was the sound of a gentle whisper.*
I KINGS 19:12 TLB

The Spirit of God is gentle and kind. He's
not in the chaos of our day, but in the quiet
moments when we can hear our hearts. We
need to find more whispering moments.
They're the ones that bring us back to life, to
the things that matter most, to what's right in
front of us, needing His love.

*Father, quiet my heart to hear You today,
so I can see the hearts that need Your love.*

We have received God's Spirit...so we can know
the wonderful things God has freely given us.
I CORINTHIANS 2:12 NLT

Jesus paid for our freedom and the wonderful things God freely gives. Grace is overwhelming for a reason—it's much too good to keep to ourselves. Give some away today. Give a little love to every person you see. Give kindness every chance you get. Give your time to someone in need, even though it interrupts your plan. Our plans will never be more important than the chances God gives us to share His love.

Father, show me the way to show Your grace to
the world, and help me see every chance You give.

Yet I am confident I will see the Lord's goodness...
PSALM 27:13 NLT

God is for us every moment of every day. What happens is for our good. There will be some days, and sometimes many in a row, that tempt us to question Him and how everything in our lives will be worked into good. But it's truth and He is truly good. Stay confident in your faith and in His promises. In time they both bring what's best.

Lord, I'm confident that Your goodness is sure and Your promises are true.

O God, my heart is quiet and confident.
No wonder I can sing Your praises!
PSALM 57:7 TLB

A quiet heart when the world around us is loud and demanding—God, give us Your grace for the challenge. Be the still, small voice that gives us confidence again that You're in control of all the earth and the universe holding us in place. We're so small here…and You're so magnificent. Keep us in the palm of Your hand today and remind us, in the depths of our souls, that we always will be.

Father, my heart will be all-in today,
trusting You with all that is.

...God sees into my heart right now.
I CORINTHIANS 13:12 TLB

Now is what matters. Always. We can't see ahead, and we can't change what's behind, but God can. Not only is He pulling our hearts in the direction of His best, He's taking the past, when we fell out of step with His will, and turning it into something good—a stronger soul, a deeper understanding of grace. With God, all is good now, or it will be. We just live the moments and *trust*.

Father, keep my heart close to You today,
on the path of Your perfect will.

I am poor and weak, yet the Lord is thinking
about me right now! O my God, You are
my helper. You are my Savior...
PSALM 40:17 TLB

Help us, Lord, in every weak moment, when
we forget the strength of our Savior and
the truth of Your constant attention to our
every need. You see them and You see *us*.
Even when we feel there must be a mistake
in Your timing...there never is. You are all
sufficiency, in all things, at all times, and in
perfect timing.

Father, You are my strength today in every moment,
giving Your full attention to my every need.

JUNE 27

*...We can have real peace with Him because of
what Jesus Christ our Lord has done for us.*
ROMANS 5:1 TLB

Real peace with God...what a perfect way to
start the day. Let your worries roll into that
peace and wash away for these daylight hours.
He's in control of every moment, and they
are *all* in the best interest of His loving plan
for you.

*Lord, You are my peace, and Your plan for
me is as good and loving as You are.*

*...You are a letter from Christ... It is not a letter
written with pen and ink, but by the Spirit of the living
God; not one carved on stone, but in human hearts.*
II CORINTHIANS 3:3 TLB

Our lives are letters penned by the pierced
hands holding our moments. A beautiful
set of words about love and redemption and
grace—His life in us, making our lives new.
And today He's going to keep rewriting broken
lives through us, through the kindness, love,
and hope we share.

*Lord, let me be a love letter from
You to every life I touch today.*

Search me, O God, and know my heart;
try me, and know my anxieties.
PSALM 139:23 NKJV

They're here, the anxieties. The pressures of life pressing down on us while we fight to stand strong and get our hearts ready for another day. We can't do it alone and we never have to. Heart-readiness is God's specialty—and He's got all the courage, confidence, and calm we need today.

Father, make my heart strong today,
confident in Your constant love and care.

Bless the Lord who is my immovable Rock...
PSALM 144:1 TLB

We have an immovable Rock in this fast-moving world, where our lives speed forward with no slow-down in sight—a sea of lists and loudness and not enough time in a day. Jesus holds us steady and grounds us in love, the calming, peaceful promise of love no matter what we do or don't accomplish, even if we make a mess of giving out the love He's giving us. We are secure and loved—*always*.

Father, Your love for me is rock-solid and faithful.
Thank You for immovable, immeasurable grace.

What a wonderful God we have…the source of every mercy, and the One who so wonderfully comforts and strengthens us in our hardships and trials.
II CORINTHIANS 1:3 TLB

From pain emerges a deeper trust in God, a beauty we couldn't imagine would come out of the suffering we didn't feel ready for or strong enough to handle. But God keeps a tighter grip on us when it gets hard for us to stand, because He won't let us fall. And in those close-knit moments, trust is digging deep and taking hold, making it impossible to shake loose for anything that lies ahead.

Father, I put my trust in You for whatever is and is to be.

*...Be sure of this—that I am with you
always, even to the end of the world.*
MATTHEW 28:20 TLB

He is with you and He is greater—greater than
the doubts that defy His provision, greater
than the circumstances that challenge His
hope. He's greater than anything that comes
at you today, and that means you're going to
get through it with guts and grace. Be sure
of this: because of Him you're as brave as
it takes.

*Father, I believe You're greater than
all my fears today and with me to
walk through whatever comes.*

*Now You've got my feet on the life path, all
radiant from the shining of Your face. Ever since
You took my hand, I'm on the right way.*
PSALM 61:11 THE MESSAGE

The path of our life is as original as we
are—and the pathway lighting came on the
moment we gave our lives to God. Now
we've got a walking companion too. He knows
the best way to joy, peace, hope, love—all the
best stuff for our souls. It's impossible to get
there, really *anywhere* good, without sticking by
His side. And, truly, since our hearts found
grace, there isn't any place we'd rather be.

*Father, take my hand today and show me
the way to every good thing it holds.*

You are who you are through this gift
and call of Jesus Christ...
ROMANS 1:7 THE MESSAGE

We couldn't see our true selves until we met our true Savior and saw our *absolute* need for Him. How does a heart make it through this battle-torn earth journey without Him? Our hearts just weren't made for it. That's why our first call is love. Simply, always love. Be the love connection from heaven to here—right where you are today...to who you are with today...however Jesus leads.

Lord, help me love others the way You love me.

...Now we have a far better hope, for Christ makes us acceptable to God, and now we may draw near to Him.
HEBREWS 7:19 TLB

Let your faith ignite your dreams. If your hope is in Christ, it's on a course to come true. Your dream is tied to your gift, and every gift you have came from Him. Time is simply God preparing your heart for more than you dared to imagine.

Father, my hope is in You for the dreams my heart holds.

*...Let us run with endurance the race God has set
before us. We do this by keeping our eyes on Jesus,
the champion who initiates and perfects our faith...*
HEBREWS 12:1—2 NLT

Life moves at an out-of-breath pace sometimes. There's more tripping over the hurdles and pulling ourselves back up than we'd like to admit. There are days when we see our Champion at every turn and days when He seems to fall silent. Keep going. Keep being brave, because even when fears and falls make us feel forgotten, we never are. Jesus is in every step, perfecting our faith for His perfect will.

*Lord, thank You for being my strength
and my Champion with every step.*

*Since we have a great High Priest who has
entered heaven, Jesus the Son of God, let
us hold firmly to what we believe.*

HEBREWS 4:14 NLT

The meaning in our moments, days, and lives
will never be fully revealed to us on our earthly
journey. We can't see the hearts of others and
how our actions affect them. We're not doing
the eternal, heart-changing work; God is.
We pray, surrender, and stay close to Him,
but only He can see how the love He pours
through is creating a heavenly tidal wave. One
day we will *see*—today we will *serve*.

*Lord, help me serve others with love today,
knowing Your reflection can change a heart.*

*I am the vine, you are the branches. He who
abides in Me, and I in him, bears much fruit;
for without me you can do nothing.*
JOHN 15:5 NKJV

He's always here with us, abiding. We're a part
of Him and He's going to give us the joy
we need to stay strong and the love we need
to give away. He's happy to be the love we
need, because we need to feel it too, and
He understands. So let's get still for a few
moments and soak in His infinite, incredible
love. It'll fill our hearts full for whatever
comes our way today.

*Father, I know I can't give without letting
You fill my heart, so I'm asking You to.*

God knew what He was doing from the
very beginning.... We see the original and
intended shape of our lives there in Him.
ROMANS 8:29 THE MESSAGE

The shape of our lives in Him is one that
shapes the world with love. It's what He's
made of and why He made us. And isn't His
true and unconditional love the best thing?
We don't always get it right here, on the human
side. But God's love for us doesn't change or
shift because of our moods or mistakes. He
loves us today and every other day because we
belong to Him.

Father, I know that You love me completely
and my life is complete in You.

Thank You for making me so wonderfully complex!
It is amazing to think about…
PSALM 139:14 TLB

Created in God's image, yet we're all so distinctly different. You are incredibly special; do you think about that often enough? No one else on earth takes the same path you do, but God makes sure you cross paths with exactly the right people—the ones meant to be in your story. Love the souls in your story today…and give a little of God's love to the ones who pass through.

Father, every person You created wants to know
Your love. Let me bring it into the world today.

JULY 11

...Oh, the joys of those who put their trust in Him!
PSALM 2:12 TLB

Every moment of the day—hat's when you matter to God. That's when He's working together the details of all you've gone through, and all you're going through, for good. His hand penned the pages of your life and His hand is holding you while you live them. Live them with joy.

*Father, trusting You with all my heart is
the only way to live with real joy.*

Search the book of the Lord and see all that
He will do; not one detail will He miss...
ISAIAH 34:16 TLB

We serve a God of details. He numbers the
hairs on our head and collects the tears that
fall. Not a moment of our day goes unnoticed
or left to chance. What's supposed to get done
today will get done; where we're supposed to
be, we'll be. The best way to peace is to let God
set the pace—and trust Him with the plan.

Father, I trust every moment to Your plan
today, accepting the steps with peace of heart.

*...Be rich in good works...give happily to
those in need, always be ready to share with
others whatever God has given...*
I TIMOTHY 6:18 TLB

It's easy to feel as if our routines aren't where
God is working. He can't possibly be doing
eternal business through the mundane things
we do every day. But unless you're deliberately
spending time in solitude, you're going to get
the chance to speak a kind word, encourage a
heart, love, and love some more. Everything
we do as a child of God is touching eternity
with every moment that we serve Him.

*Father, I give my hands to the work of Your
will, with a full and thankful heart.*

*...I refresh the humble and give new courage
to those with repentant hearts.*
ISAIAH 57:15 TLB

Sunlight breaks on a new day and a world of brokenness. There are hearts that have been hoping long...rejected again...afraid too much of the time. God sees each one. Not one soul slips through the cracks of His care. He has new courage for us today, with refreshing promises: I am with you. I will rescue you. I will uphold you with My victorious right hand.

Father, I trust You to be my strength today.

Every day of my life was recorded in Your book. Every moment was laid out before a single day had passed.
PSALM 139:16 NLT

Moments are gifts, and moments displaced by fear steal our joy! God is the architect of our days and His plans were set before we took our first breath. It's hard to comprehend that He laid out our lives in such detail, but He did. Let's enjoy today and remember: our moments are written, our God isfaithful, and absolutely nothing is more powerful than the love in the design.

Father, My moments are sketched by Your hand. I'll live each one with thankfulness and trust.

Commit your work to the Lord, then it will succeed.
PROVERBS 16:3 TLB

All things for Him, always. God makes everything we put in His hands or do in His name succeed. It might not be by the world's measure and we might not see the reward this side of heaven, but if God promises promotion, it's better than anything our hearts could ask for or imagine.

Father, I commit the work of my hands to You
and thank You for the reward Your love brings.

*Don't be afraid, I've redeemed you. I've
called your name. You're mine.*
ISAIAH 43:2 THE MESSAGE

Fear will not win today. God has your hand
and He's holding the plan that is best for you.
He's redeemed you with a love so powerful
it puts every fear to rest and every doubt to
silence. Give God your day and watch His
strength prevail. He'll be watching you win.

*Lord, You are my hope and my tower of strength.
I praise You for defeating every fear with Your love.*

...Tell the world how wonderful He is.
PSALM 66:2 TLB

There are a million ways our lives can tell the world about His love. There are 86,400 seconds in a single day. Let's use as many as we can to reflect His joy, His love, His kind heart, His saving grace, His everlasting hope, His gentleness, His generosity, His patience, His forgiveness, and how about what He's done for us—and in us. A lifetime won't be enough to show how wonderful He is, but we can spend our lifetime trying.

Father, let me be mindful of You in every
moment today so the world can catch
a glimpse of the beauty of You.

Come, see the glorious things God has done. What marvelous miracles happen to His people!

PSALM 66:5 TLB

The glory of God is magnificent in the moments—and sometimes the most ordinary become the most radiant. When a child smiles back at you, their eyes so full of wonder, so filled with their Creator's light… When the sunset looks like a thousand shades of pink… When something you hope for comes sweetly and silently, between you and God alone… Look for His glory in the little things today… and thank Him for the view.

Father, Your glory shines through the big joys in the smallest moments. Open my eyes to see it today.

May He grant you according to your heart's desire, and fulfill all your purpose.
PSALM 20:4 NKJV

God makes no mistakes in orchestrating our life and purpose. The desire of His heart is for us to follow the desire of ours—because He put it there. Our dreams align with our gifts, every good gift comes from Him, and what you do today is one more step of the way.

Father, let the desires You've given to me bring glory to You, and help me pursue them with all my heart.

For we are God's masterpiece. He has created
us anew in Christ Jesus, so we can do the
good things He planned for us long ago.
EPHESIANS 2:10 NLT

God's faithfulness is in every sunrise, every moment, and every season. Our days come and go by what His heart plans and His hand guides. Not one of the days He gives should be lived with fear or failure. What might look like a mess to us will become a part of the masterpiece He's making of our lives in Him.

Father, I'm the work of Your hand and
my life is sculpted by Your love.

*...He is the faithful God who keeps His covenant
for a thousand generations and lavishes His
unfailing love on those who love Him...*
DEUTERONOMY 7:9 NLT

Love lavished and unfailing—on every moment of our days and all the days of our lives. I don't know how it can be any better than that. It feels amazing to be loved, and how do we know we are? Through kindness, and through being preferred, favored, valued, and cared for. That's God toward you, in a measure beyond belief.

*Father, Your fathomless love for
me fills my heart with joy.*

My hands have made both heaven and earth;
they and everything in them are mine...
ISAIAH 66:2 NLT

You are never alone. You are never ignored.
God is paying close attention to everything
that concerns you: the heartbreaking, the
happy, and every moment in between. There's
nothing easy about life unless we ease into the
cradling of His hand and rest there...trust
there...and realize we *belong* there.

Father, I'll rest in You and Your constant love,
knowing all my days are in Your hand.

O Lord my God, many and many a time
you have done great miracles for us, and
we are ever in Your thoughts...
PSALM 40:5 TLB

God's thinking about you as you start the day, hoping you see the good things running through it, the ways His love is all over it, and how infinitely valuable you are to Him. He's going to be guiding your steps, so let your heart be peaceful and your smile full of joy and your spirit all kinds of thankful, because with God in control, it's going to be a *great* day.

Father, I give my day to You from start to finish. I'll
rest in trust and be thankful for Your constant love.

The counsel of the LORD stands forever,
the plans of His heart to all generations.
PSALM 33:11 NKJV

God has planned, with a heart of love and mercy, each of our days. Not a single moment takes Him by surprise. Every step we take sinks into the security of His love and grace. Don't think about what can go wrong. You're in the right hands. And it's all going to work out—and fit together for your good.

Lord, make my steps take the
way of Your will today.

For I know the thoughts that I think toward
you, says the LORD, thoughts of peace…
to give you a future and a hope.
JEREMIAH 29:11 NKJV

A peaceful heart is the way God's Spirit leads us. Even in the middle of tough days with tensions tugging on every side, we can learn to turn to Him. Peace comes through trust—trusting the battle is His, not ours…knowing He's in control, no matter what…believing that what's in front of us is filtered through His love and will be fine-tuned for our good.

Father, every plan You have for me is for the good
of my heart and for growing my trust in You.

*How joyful are those who fear the
LORD—all who follow His ways!*
PSALM 128:1 NLT

There's a difference between joy and just being happy. Joy is an inside job only God can do. Happiness feels good but is fleeting because it rides on our emotions. Choose joy. Let God make you stronger every time it gets rough and you smile through, knowing that whatever is pulling you down is pulling you away from your joy-source—and you choose not to let it happen.

*Father, when I choose Your joy,
I get Your strength.*

How exquisite Your love, O God! How
eager we are to run under your wings.
PSALM 36:7 THE MESSAGE

Watchful, attentive, overwhelming, and over
us always is God's exquisite love. We run to
it on hard days when our hearts are worn
out, because He never tires of holding us.
His wings of mercy lift us up as many times
as we weary from the weights of life sometimes difficult to live. In Him we find new
strength to fill our hearts with fuel to go on—
and a mighty love to move us forward.

Father, Your love is my shelter and
the salvation of my heart.

Let Your favor shine on Your servant...
PSALM 31:16 NLT

Let God's favor shine on us today, His grace bringing so much good that our hearts gush with gratefulness. How can that not-of-this-world love be in us and not inspire us to take every step with joy and touch every life with kindness? Make the moments mindful of giving: all that we can of Him for all that He's done for us.

Father, thank You for Your favor on my
life and for loving me so faithfully.

I will praise You as long as I live, lifting
up my hands to You in prayer.
PSALM 63:4 NLT

We lift our hands in prayer and God scoops
us up in His love, a love that listens to every
word we speak and hears our hearts calling
from within. Prayer is a privilege, a place of
refuge, and a powerful force. It's the best way
to start our day—and the way to make our day
the best it can be.

Father, I praise You for the privilege of
prayer and the power of Your love.

What is the price of two sparrows—one copper coin?
But not a single sparrow can fall to the ground without
your Father knowing it. And the very hairs on your
head are all numbered. So don't be afraid; you are
more valuable to God than a whole flock of sparrows.

MATTHEW 10:29–31 NLT

Nothing in this world or beyond can diminish
your worth to God. Don't let circumstances
diminish His light in you. Build your strength
by bringing His joy to everything you're going
through. There's no way He's leaving your
side or your struggle, and His love-filled
response is coming soon.

Father, I stand with joy in the center
of my circumstances, trusting Your
love to carry me through.

...Now you have light from the Lord.
So live as people of light!
EPHESIANS 5:8 NLT

We know Your light is in us, Lord. It helps us
to see into the lives that are in need, and not
only see but *do*. The brilliance of Your love
leads us to be compassionate and willing to go
out of our way and out of our comfort zone
to serve—to be love, light, and life-changers.

Lord, let me shine Your light into every
place and every life by sharing Your love.

...Continue to rely on the grace of God.
ACTS 13:43 NLT

By grace alone we press on, find peace, and move forward. It's the hardest thing to do sometimes, to forget what hurt us so badly. But that's what grace is so good at—helping us see that forgiveness is for all people and all things, no matter how fierce the wound or how far the fall.

Father, thank You for the grace You give without limits, and for teaching my heart to give it too.

I can do all things through Christ who strengthens me.
PHILIPPIANS 4:13 NKJV

This is the promise we lean on so many days because God promises strength for *all* things. When it feels like we can't handle another thing or take another step, Jesus steps in. And we remember: what we're going through can't compare to what He's gone through—and He did it all for us.

Lord, You are my source
of strength in all things.

...I will protect you, and your reward will be great.
GENESIS 15:1 NLT

Our great God promises to give us a great reward—for us, that reward is Jesus—and it doesn't get any higher, brighter, or better. What He went through because He loves us gives us strength to get through *anything*. Earthly trials can't defeat us because there's a King at the right hand of God who defends us. Live today with the confidence won by perfect love, knowing you're loved perfectly.

Father, thank You for the love of Jesus, our greatest reward.

…You live under the freedom of God's grace.
ROMANS 6:14 NLT

It's an incredible freedom, forgiveness. God forgives—and gives His unconditional love and favor too. Our hearts and minds will never grasp the magnitude of it all. And yet, it's ours. We're loved today…favored today…forgiven today…and hopefully we're thankful, joyful, hopeful, and kind—to show our love in return.

Father, Your grace is great and more
than enough to fill my heart with.

...We are all saved the same way, by the
undeserved grace of the Lord Jesus.
ACTS 15:11 NLT

Today is a brand-new start. The slate is clean
and God's grace is here to greet us. Walking
in grace reminds us that every one of our
torn-apart hearts is in need of the perfect
One—and not one of us has done anything to
deserve the love and forgiveness of Jesus. Let's
see everyone through the lens of His love...
and let our lives become a clearer reflection
of His grace.

Father, we belong to You because of
what Jesus did. Help us walk in Your
grace and reflect our Savior today.

*...Worship and serve Him with a clean heart
and a willing mind, for the Lord sees every heart
and understands and knows every thought...*
I CHRONICLES 28:9 TLB

God alone knows the intention of our hearts; that's why our hearts must intentionally love. There will be emotional trip-ups and roadblocks, but we can never allow our emotions to extinguish the love that transformed us—because His love is the love the world needs to see.

Father, make me a mirror of Your love today.

God is our refuge and strength,
a tested help in times of trouble.
PSALM 46:1 TLB

God is the heart's refuge and the soul's
courage. In everything that tests our faith
and hope today, God is our tested and
trustworthy help. He will not fail us if we call
on Him, because He's called into action by
His unfailing love—and no power on earth or
beyond can slow it or stop it from reaching us.

Father, I trust the saving power of Your
love in every test and trial that comes.

...If you seek Him, He'll make sure you find Him...
I CHRONICLES 28:9 THE MESSAGE

You're going to be God's love to someone today. The path of your life is about the people in your life—hearts needing and seeking the gift of love. Give it freely, joyfully, kindly. Don't give up on giving it, no matter how hard it gets, and know that when you need it, He's always there.

Father, let me give Your love generously
today to every heart I touch.

*Ah, Lord GOD! Behold, You have made the heavens
and the earth by Your great power and outstretched
arm. There is nothing too hard for You.*
JEREMIAH 32:17 NKJV

You're going to get through it all today. That
thing that's got you stressed…that waiting for
what you've been hoping for…that person
with a hurting heart that fell short of being
kind to you. God's watching your day and
holding you close and turning all the rough
spots into opportunities to lean on Him
and walk in love. And you're going to do it—
because He's helping you through it.

*Father, thank You for being my strength and
patience today as I walk in Your love.*

*...He set my feet on solid ground and
steadied me as I walked along.*
PSALM 40:2 NLT

God's got you today—on the solid ground of
His love and the steady path of your purpose.
Nothing that happens is going to destroy the
good things He has planned for you. If there's
a detour, He's already seen it and made a way
around it. If you slip, He's there to catch you.
Take your steps with confidence. God's in
control of each one.

*Father, You're ahead of me and behind
me, guiding my steps with Your love.*

...Let Your compassion quickly meet our needs...
PSALM 79:8 NLT

God is the strength that sustains us, the compassion that carries us, and the love that changes us—and we need Him every moment of every day. We're quick to fall short in our weaknesses, yet He's quick to meet needs in His compassion. Our hearts can't fully understand that astonishing love, but we will *always* have it.

Father, You're full of compassion toward my needs, and Your love is what I need most.

Go after a life of love as if your life
depended on it—because it does...
I CORINTHIANS 14:1 THE MESSAGE

Good moments—*God moments*—are the ones
that happen when we're busy putting others
first. That's what love does. *Always.* Much of
the beauty of selfless giving is the overflow of
love returned. The habit of choosing to love
creates a deep well of His love within us...at
the ready to draw from and give away again.

Lord, let me love without hesitation today and
trust You to be my strength in every moment.

God, who began the good work within you, will
continue His work until it is finally finished
on the day when Christ Jesus returns.
PHILIPPIANS 1:6 NLT

Let God's strength renew your confidence to face your day with courage. All is good or for your good. That won't change or falter, because God won't. His work is steady and sure. He doesn't take breaks in working out what's best for your life. It's a continuous act of His love—because He loves you, breath by breath.

Father, thank You for loving me in moments
and doing Your good work within me.

Let no one seek his own,
but each one the other's well-being.
1 CORINTHIANS 10:24 NKJV

In every single moment of your life, God is orchestrating what is best for your well-being. Be well today! Lean into love, look for the need, and seek the good of those around you. God will turn your kind words and loving actions into blessings—so be ready for the pure joy that love brings, because God is going to give it!

Father, You're working things together
for the wonder of eternity. Let my
life light the way with love!

…Your strength shall be renewed
day by day like morning dew.
PSALM 110:3 TLB

New strength for a new day—that's a promise to believe and be thankful for. We don't always have leftover courage to carry us if there have been too many days of fighting hard to believe and crying tears of disappointment and holding on with slipping hands. But God knew when He created us that we'd need new hope daily. So here it is: all the hope and strength you need today, straight from His almighty hand.

Father, Your strength is new and Your love is
faithful. Thank You for being all I need.

...His faithful promises are your armor.
PSALM 91:4 TLB

It can't be taken from you or broken through. God's armor isn't made on earth, but it can shield our hearts from the darkness here. He gives comfort to the grieving and hope to the hurting. He gives joy to the discouraged and strength to the fearful. And the greatest barrier we have in *any* battle is the power of His love for us.

Father, I trust in Your faithfulness
and the power of Your love.

AUGUST 18

The life of the godly is full of life and joy.
PROVERBS 13:9 NLT

Light up the day with joy. Smile through.
You're light in this world because God ignited
your spirit with love—and there's nothing
worth the worry when God has won the fight.
Soak in the moments that you know He gives:
little things that make you happy or the sound
of laughter from the voices you love. Being in
love with God means being in love with the
life He gives.

*Father, open my eyes to see the joy in my
moments, and let my life be a light in the world.*

A desire accomplished is sweet to the soul...
PROVERBS 13:19 NKJV

Our hearts are going to need some never-give-up on the way to our dreams. God sees them and He'll be faithful to see them through; we just need to trust and surrender to His timing. The greatest part of His timing? It's always in line with His best.

Father, I trust You with the desires of my heart.
I know Your best comes in Your timing.

When You grant a blessing, O LORD,
it is an eternal blessing!
1 CHRONICLES 17:27 NLT

What God gives, our hearts need most. His love most of all. We're saved by it, secure in it, and called to share it. If we love Him first, loving others will become second nature to us—a characteristic almost instinctive because we do it so often. Practice love today, toward every heart, in every situation, and know that when you do, you bring a glimpse of eternity to earth.

Father, Your love is the greatest blessing of
all. Let it shine through my life today.

I pray that your hearts will be flooded with light so that you can understand the confident hope He has given to those He called…
EPHESIANS 1:18 NLT

Lord, shed Your light on the hope in our hearts today. Help us understand how unfailing it is, even when our souls are weary from the wait and worn from the waves crashing against us. Hope rests in Your hands…and our answers in Your timing.

Father, fill my heart with hope and light. I trust in You alone.

I will be your God through all your lifetime, yes, even when your hair is white with age. I made you and I will care for you. I will carry you along and be your Savior.
ISAIAH 46:4 TLB

You are loved perfectly, forgiven completely, and cared for constantly. God won't quit you. When it feels like a lonely journey at times, this life in Him, know that He quietly carries you forward to the purposes up ahead—and they are *always* good.

Father, I'll let my heart rest in You today, confident in Your care...carried by Your love.

...I have loved you...with an everlasting love.
With unfailing love I have drawn you to Myself.
JEREMIAH 31:3 NLT

A new day begins, and God's love draws us in. Not by fear or force, but by loving us first and fully. There are no empty places in the vastness of His love—like the sky above and the air around. Let it fill you and hold you and heal you. And know it will *never* leave you.

Father, Your love is my constant
comfort and strength.

The Lord God who created the heavens and stretched them out...gives life and breath and spirit to everyone...
ISAIAH 42:5 TLB

God's hand paints the sunrise across the horizon and we see the first light of new mercy. We don't have to carry the weight of yesterday or drag our past mistakes behind us—even when our minds won't let go. Jesus broke the grip of guilt by becoming the greatest sacrifice. So take hold of the gift of today with both hands and all your heart. Love is giving you a brand-new start.

Father, thank You for giving new mercies and new beginnings through the power of Jesus's sacrificial love.

Show me Your strong love in wonderful ways...
PSALM 17:7 TLB

God is the strong love in our weak moments—
when our patience is gone and we feel low on
good things to give or kindness to show. He
is more than enough, and His endless supply
is a whisper away. Take a deep breath and say
a short prayer and know that no matter what
the day holds, God is everything we need.

Father, Your love is my source, my
security, and my strength.

Let everything alive give praises to the Lord!...
PSALM 150:6 TLB

Let our quiet moments breathe His praise, let our trembling, tired, tested times breathe His praise, let our joy within and our tears coming out breathe His praise. It's the thankfulness in it that sets us right when everything else goes wrong. It's the love exchange between our heart and His that holds us up when we can't stand any longer. Rejoicing in Him recharges us—and it's always a breath away.

Father, I thank You and praise You for being there to love—and for breathing strength back into me.

Give generously...not grudgingly, for the LORD
your God will bless you in everything you do.
DEUTERONOMY 15:10 NLT

Whatever God has for your hands to do
today, put your heart into it too. Give it to
God, and give it your all. There won't be a
single regret in the moments you choose to
serve Him. Love will be in them, patience will
prevail, and somewhere in there a heart will
be blessed because you're being a blessing.

Father, I commit the work of
my hands to You today.

...All have the same Lord who generously gives
His riches to all those who ask Him for them.
ROMANS 10:12 TLB

No measurement on earth can determine the riches God gives, and our hearts can't fully contain them. That's how it is with eternal things, *God* things. There isn't a single material aspect about them, but they *materialize* in abundant, full, and everlasting life. It's amazing to think it's as simple as asking, but it is. Ask Him for what your heart needs today— and open it wide for the overflow.

Father, fill my heart with the riches of Your grace.
It makes the blessings of life even sweeter.

*Be generous with your lives. By opening up to
others, you'll prompt people to open up with
God, this generous Father in heaven.*
MATTHEW 5:16 THE MESSAGE

If we think for a moment that we're the only
ones hurting, all alone in the thick of it, trying to find our way out, we're believing a
lie...and it didn't come from our Life Giver.
God knows we need each other because He
created us to help each other—and opening
our hearts to help helps us heal too.

*Father, You're the perfect Helper and
Healer. Give me the courage to open
my heart to others who need You.*

…Give yourselves to the gifts God gives you…
I CORINTHIANS 14:1 THE MESSAGE

Stir up your gifts today and let God use them. There are always ways, and they come through God-directed opportunities in our day. He builds our lives according to His plan, and the unique traits you have were designed to be used right now, right where you are—bringing blessings to others and glory to Him.

Father, I surrender my gifts to Your glory and Your guiding.

God blesses those who patiently endure testing and temptation. Afterward they will receive the crown of life that God has promised to those who love Him.
JAMES 1:12 NLT

Trials lead to a closer relationship with God and become a threshold for even greater blessings in our lives—and deeper intimacy with Him is the greatest gift among them. Drawing nearer to the One who puts us first and loves us most is sweetness in our struggles that leads to the strengthening of our souls.

Father, being near to You is being blessed in fullest measure.

SEPTEMBER 1

*You can show others the goodness of God, for He
called you out of the darkness into His wonderful light.*
I PETER 2:9 NLT

Stand in the unwavering confidence that you
can do anything God calls you to do today, and
believe it will be blessed. His light in you is
now a beacon for others who are searching…
hoping…hurting. Shine the goodness of the
One who called you and saved you, who
carries you and cares for you—and let His love
keep lighting the world.

*Father, show the world around me that Your love
is within me, and let Your light shine ever brighter.*

...I have trusted in the LORD without wavering.
PSALM 26:1 ESV

Trust Him today. Give God all the stuff you weren't created to carry: the fear, the stress, the worries. When we've done all we can to try to fix what we couldn't do without Him from the beginning, it's time to leave every care at His feet and rest. Breathe in His peace and let every doubt out. He's taken care of it all.

Lord, I trust You with the cares that have carried me away from You, and I praise You for Your provision.

*I pray that Christ will be more and more at home in
your hearts, living within you as you trust in Him...*
EPHESIANS 3:17 TLB

Our hearts, Christ's home—it's amazing to
think about. The love that sacrificed all and
shook the earth lives within us, His created.
We can't hold it all and we aren't meant to. It's
within us to work out the wonders of grace and
to give away generously every moment that we
can. It's all that matters for every reason—the
love of Jesus. Thank God for another day of
giving it away.

*Lord, Your love is more than my heart will
ever hold. Give me every chance to share it.*

*...May your roots go down deep into
the soil of God's marvelous love.*
EPHESIANS 3:17 TLB

Let our hearts dig deep today to absorb our life-giving water. In God's love we grow more beautiful as He makes our lives more fruitful. It's the sweetest to bear, all that comes from Him into the world—and it produces the greatest amount of hope and healing.

*Father, I want the roots of my heart planted
securely in Your love so that all I give to
others comes from the beauty of You.*

Lord, when doubts fill my mind, when my heart is in turmoil, quiet me and give me renewed hope and cheer.

PSALM 94:19 TLB

Be blessed with a quiet heart today. God is taking care of everything, including our moments. They come and go so quickly, but if we invite Him into all of them, they add up to a whole lot of love in a day. And isn't that what makes our lives more memorable: more, and more, and *more* love? I pray you know He loves you, right now and always, and I hope it fills your heart with hope.

Lord, with a quiet heart, my hope is in You.

A peaceful heart leads to a healthy body…
PROVERBS 14:30 NLT

A peaceful heart in a noisy world and a busy life—we're going to need to lean into God for that today. He loves us and heals us inside and out, and staying calm in the chaos keeps our hearts *well*. There isn't a thing we can do to change the things only He can, so we'll just trust Him moment by moment and cling to His peace through it all.

Lord, all that comes to steal
my peace I give to You.

...Oh, the joys of those who put their trust in Him!
PSALM 2:12 TLB

Joy comes from a deep-seated trust that God is in control of everything in our lives. Not a moment goes by without His attention. We're held carefully in the palm of His hand, our names inscribed there too. He won't forget us, no matter how many times we fall away or let worries come between our trust and His faithfulness. So stir up the joy and trust Him today. His love won't fail you.

Father, Your joy is my strength in every moment. Let my heart trust in You always.

The Lord will guide you continually,
and satisfy you with all good things…
ISAIAH 58:11 TLB

God guides all your moments with love, and all your moments are leading to good things. Trusting Him will not disappoint, and loving Him will satisfy *every* need. Today is one step closer to the things your heart desires—and strength in you that you've never known before.

Lord, You guide my steps with love and cover
me with grace. I trust in You alone.

Because He bends down and listens,
I will pray as long as I breathe!
PSALM 116:2 TLB

The greater our need, the more God shows Himself strong. There's nothing in heaven or on earth greater than Him and His love for us. He listens and hears the cries of our hearts, bending down to meet us where we are. When prayers are whispered, God is willing—and His provision will come at the perfect time.

Father, thank You for hearing my voice and coming to my side. Your love is my refuge and hope.

...Fill all who love You with Your happiness.
PSALM 5:11 TLB

If we want to be truly happy, we have to keep our focus on love—God's love *for* us and God's love *through* us. We weren't created to go it alone, and since we need each other, we need to help each other. Let's do some things today in the spirit of love...and get ready to have a happy heart.

Lord, Your love makes me happy...
to have and to give.

Let my soul be at rest again, for the
LORD has been good to me.
PSALM 116:7 NLT

Some rest in the goodness of God sounds like a great plan for the day. Even if it gets a little crazy on the outside, there's a quiet on the inside that can't be shaken. It's anchored in the One who's anchored our souls in everlasting hope. He's *been* good to us and He'll *be* good to us—and that will never change.

Lord, be the peace in my soul and the
hope in my circumstances. I'll rest in
the promise of Your goodness.

...Let the whole earth be filled with His glory...
PSALM 72:19 NKJV

Everything for God's glory. If we could live every moment by those words, we could change the world with His love. His love has changed us immeasurably. It's made us new and whole. And the more we love Him, the more we understand the magnitude of the grace His love made possible.

Father, let my actions and
words bring glory to You.

…There shall be showers, showers of blessing…
EZEKIEL 34:26 TLB

If we could see the blessings God has prepared for us, we'd see that what we're walking through now is preparing our hearts to receive them. We don't want what our hearts aren't ready for—and no one knows our hearts better than the One who created them.

Father, prepare my heart for the blessings You have for me. I trust in Your love and Your timing.

We live with(in) the shadow of the Almighty,
sheltered by the God who is above all gods.
PSALM 91:1 TLB

God is our shelter. Our place of peace when it's
hectic here in the world, when nothing seems
in order. We can go to Him, any moment of
any day, and find the quiet our hearts need.
We can sit and be loved, no guilt…just grace.
And if it's what you need right now, there's no
waiting in line—only open arms to greet you.

Father, You're my shelter in any
storm, any time of day or night.

Give us help for the hard task;
in God we'll do our very best.
PSALM 108:12–13 THE MESSAGE

Sometimes there are too many hard days in a row and it feels like too much for our hearts to take. But anything that takes more than the strength we have leads us to the One we need. God is the strength of our hearts and our constant help. He's never too busy to love us through the tough stuff.

Father, thank You for always being there with
love and strength to help me through.

Blessed is the Lord, for He has shown me that
His never-failing love protects me...
PSALM 31:21 TLB

A love to count on...one that never brings up
the past, doesn't fear the future, and stands
ready to bless us in the present. God's love is
what we need right now, this moment, to walk
in the purpose He has for our lives. We won't
fail if we depend on the love that won't fail us.

Lord, I live in the protection of Your unfailing
love. Guide me in the path of Your purpose.

SEPTEMBER 17

...Think about all you can
praise God for and be glad about.
PHILIPPIANS 4:8 TLB

To begin with: a love so vast it can't be measured...a hope so sure it never disappoints...and grace so beautiful it's beyond our comprehension. We think about all we can praise God for—and we know a lifetime won't be enough. It doesn't have to be, because every blessing He gives is eternal, and we have all eternity to praise Him.

Father, Your blessings are worthy of all
my praise, for all of time and beyond.

...I will trust the promises of God...
PSALM 56:3 TLB

The sunrise has welcomed God's mercies again, unfailing as always. Yesterday is forgotten, today is in His hands, and tomorrow is filled with His promises. Trusting Him will get us through the moments, because He's working them all together for our good. If we look at our circumstances from a love angle, we'll see how His hand moves *everything* into place.

*Father, I trust that You're guiding my life
with Your love, and I know You'll work
all things together for the good.*

Come before Him with thankful hearts…
PSALM 95:2 TLB

Thankfulness is easy to be around. It's a good way to be, because thankful people are joyful, smiling people. God wants us to come to Him with a thankful heart, and that should be incredibly easy for us to do—all the time. If we trust that God is in control of our moments, we can relax and know that everything He allows is making our hearts strong, faithful, and more like His.

Father, my heart is filled with thanks and praise for who You are and all You've done.

You are my hiding place from every storm of life...
PSALM 32:7 TLB

I know, some days we want to curl up in God, our hiding place, and forget the storms that are blowing through our lives. But remember, God is *always* here, and the storms will have to go. In the middle of it all He's the only comfort we need, if we just trust Him until the calm comes.

Father, I trust You at all times to be my comfort and hope.

*...Christ who died, and furthermore is also
risen...makes intercession for us.*
ROMANS 8:34

Jesus is praying for you. He loves you more
than anyone else can and He knows you better
than anyone else does. He sees the things
you hope for, and your needs are before
Him constantly. His presence with you and
His prayers for you are faithful and without
fail. It doesn't matter what the day brings,
your Intercessor is at the right hand of God,
petitioning your Father for every need.

*Lord, my needs are before You and
my hope is in You alone.*

...Cheerful givers are the ones God prizes.
II CORINTHIANS 9:7 TLB

We have hearts changed by His love, and love gives happily. It can be as simple as a smile, a word of encouragement, or a hug. There are as many ways to spread the love as there are people who need it. God's love is in endless supply today, so let's open our hearts to those in need...and let Him lead.

Father, show me where Your love
is needed most today.

*...When your faith is tested, your endurance
has a chance to grow. So let it grow, for when
your endurance is fully developed, you will be
perfect and complete, needing nothing.*
JAMES 1:3–4 NLT

Spiritual growth comes from believing
that God is present and faithful in times
of suffering as well as times of joy. He put
us together and He holds us together when
our hearts are breaking and the tears fall.
The only way to endure it all is to give it all
to Him—the disappointment, the pain, the
confusion—and He'll love you through your
path to healing, growing your faith along
the way.

*Father, I will trust You at all times, with
all things. Help me hold on to You.*

He calms the storm, so that its waves are still.
PSALM 107:29 NKJV

You've spent so long hoping, waking up to fear raining down hard, and you just want to close your eyes and forget the daylight a little longer. Then hope digs in its heels and refuses to let go of God's promise to care for you and calm the storm. Whatever you're hoping for is in Him—and it's coming.

Father, I trust in You to still the storm and restore my hope. You alone are my salvation.

You have examined my heart and
know everything about me.
PSALM 139:1 NLT

We want God to know us completely, because He's the One who *loves* us completely—and knowing His love is true, no matter what, is what changes us. We're growing to love Him more and learning to love others better, and that's how our lives become beautiful.

Father, Your love is my purpose
and the joy of my heart.

Worship the Lord with the beauty of holy lives…
PSALM 96:9 TLB

Let's go through our day thinking of our actions as acts of worship, because if we belong to God, they are. Being in a constant mode of worship encourages our spirits to be constantly connected to God—and that can only result in more love reaching more lives.

Father, let my hands worship You today in the way I serve others and show them Your love.

...God will tenderly comfort you....
He will give you the strength to endure.
II CORINTHIANS 1:7 TLB

Life just comes at us some days, leaving us tired, faith-tested, and squinting to see hope in the middle of the mayhem. But we have a Father who comes *to* us, with comfort to quiet the questions and strength to stand up and keep going. And the hope we can't bear to see disappear? He's got that too. It comes alongside His promise, "I will never, *never* fail you nor forsake you" (Hebrews 13:5 TLB).

Father, my hope, my strength, and my faith is
in You. Your love and truth will carry me.

...As for others, help them to find
the Lord by being kind...
JUDE 22:23 TLB

Kindness is powerful. We don't often think of it that way, but God's loving-kindness is as vast as the heavens—and that's no wimpy thing. An act of kindness can point a heart in the direction of God's saving grace, and there's nothing greater than that in this whole, hurting world. So remember today that it's no small thing to be kind...and *be kind*.

Father, You are kind to every soul and loving
in all of Your ways—let me follow.

...God had given us cause for great joy...
NEHEMIAH 12:43 TLB

Let's go through today with great joy in our hearts. The joy that God's giving ignites in us. The kind that doesn't depend on circumstance but changes our outlook about what we're going through. Smile a lot. Laugh without holding back. Tell someone a happy story. Just be joyful—and enjoy seeing how His joy blesses others.

Father, Your love and goodness bring great joy to my heart, and today I choose to let it shine.

Oh, how grateful and thankful I am
to the Lord because He is so good…
PSALM 7:17 TLB

Grateful and thankful—good words, great
reminders…and the best way to start every
day. God gives us so many things to appreciate.
The little faces we stare into with an "I love
you"; the quiet we crave, coming at the end
of a long day; the smell of rain; the safe trip
home; the way our hearts feel knowing He
loves us no matter what. Thank You, God,
for every good thing You give.

Father, my life is filled with gifts of Your
love. I praise You for every one.

OCTOBER 1

God puts the fallen on their feet again...
PSALM 147:6 THE MESSAGE

God will put us on our feet again—every time. His love doesn't fade in and out when we fall; it's fervent and faithful and forever. If our faith in Him could hold the way He holds us, our days would be filled with peace.

Father, Your faithful love is the rock beneath my feet and the courage that helps me soar.

For I am about to do something new.
See, I have already begun…
ISAIAH 43:19 NLT

Seasons bring change, and the beauty of each one lies in the purpose God has for it. There's no questioning whether or not it's good. In time, our hearts will *know* it is. God never changes and His plan for our lives has His love in every part of it.

Father, I trust You in every season and know
that everything You do is motivated by love.

For God is good and He loves goodness…
PSALM 11:7 TLB

It isn't once in a while, occasionally, or on a whim. God is good all the time. He's good to us and good to others *through* us. Goodness is grounded in love, and His love is as good as it gets. We might question *why* in the rough moments, but there's no question that whatever God is doing in our lives right now, He's working together with a lot of love…for a lot of good.

Father, I praise You for Your goodness and grace,
and for working all things together for good.

*Give all your worries and cares to
God, for He cares about you.*
I PETER 5:7 NLT

It's all good…because He's always good. When
the worries pile up a little and our faith wears
a little thin and our hearts need a little more
hope for the day—it's all in Him. He'll take
what's hindering our hearts and give what's
healing and helpful. Love does that because
it's all love *can* do—the good, the grace-filled,
and the best.

*Father, I lay my worries down and fill
my heart with hope. Thank You for
needs met and love without end.*

OCTOBER 5

…Your Heavenly Father already knows all your needs. Seek the Kingdom of God above all else, and live righteously, and He will give you everything you need.

MATTHEW 6:32–33 NLT

Every need met…if first we seek the One who first loved us. It's hard to imagine putting anything in our lives above God's love and purpose, but the world presses hard against the faith in us and our desire to surrender all we are to all He is. One day at a time—that's how we serve God and put Him first, and how we trust He'll be everything we need.

Lord, let Your will be the first thing I seek today, and give my heart the wisdom to follow.

*...The Lord has said it, and His Spirit
will make it all come true.*
ISAIAH 34:16 TLB

When fear seeps in slowly or comes like a
downpour, the Lord says, "Don't be afraid,
I'll never leave you." When worries close in
on every side, the Lord says, "I'm thinking of
you; give all your cares to Me." When doubt
casts a shadow on our hopes, the Lord says,
"My name is the hope of all the world.

*Lord, Your words are true and Your heart
is faithful. I put my trust in You.*

OCTOBER 7

…We don't have a priest who is out of touch with our reality. He's been through weakness and testing, experienced it all—all but the sin. So let's walk right up to Him and get what He is so ready to give. Take the mercy, accept the help.

HEBREWS 4:15–16 THE MESSAGE

We can admit it: we don't always choose the right thing or take the perfect path. We get offtrack a little and give in to feelings of hopelessness, and sometimes our hearts are hurting and our faith gets lost in the pain. Jesus understands. He was tempted as we are and empathizes with our pain. He lived in our humanness to know us *fully*—and to know how to fully help us and heal us.

Lord, thank You for coming here to make me whole. Your love is my help and my healing.

*...Great is the LORD, who delights in
blessing His servant with peace!*
PSALM 35:27 NLT

It's going to take more than a rough start,
running late, or rearranging our plans to take
our peace today. God delights in giving it, so
we're going to take a few deep breaths, smile
anyway, and practice peace. If our hearts stay
calm, we stay strong.

*Lord, I'll hold onto the blessing of peace
today and keep my heart focused on You.*

I call to GOD; God will help me. At dusk, dawn,
and noon I sigh deep sighs—He hears, He rescues.
PSALM 55:16 THE MESSAGE

You're brave, blessed, watched over, and
rescued. If you call out to Him, God hears
and holds you steady. When frustration
comes, don't let it stay. Let God's peace—the
peace that passes understanding—fill your
heart, like a deep breath fills your chest, and
give it all to Him.

Father, be my peace today. When I call out
to You, quiet my heart and calm my spirit.

Rest in the Lord; wait patiently for Him to act...
PSALM 37:7 TLB

Today might not reveal the whys of what God is doing, but we can trust that in the waiting, our hearts are growing stronger. He's going to act on our behalf, and it's going to be absolute and amazing. What He makes happen isn't temporary or fleeting—it's blessing without sorrow and favor for a lifetime. So stay hopeful and wait for it, because it's going to be more than you imagined.

Lord, I will wait patiently, hope constantly, and trust You with all my heart.

OCTOBER 11

...Day by day...He does not fail...
ZEPHANIAH 3:5 NLT

God is magnificent. Flawless. Our minds can't wrap around the love, faithfulness, and power in Him—and He lives in us. When we call on Him, He will not fail us because He does not fail. Our hearts should do a victory dance every morning. knowing who's fighting for us and what His love can do. We can conquer anything today—we serve the God of *anything is possible.*

Father, You're all I need to overcome any obstacle and reach anything I hope for.

The LORD has made everything for His own purposes…
PROVERBS 16:4 NLT

His purpose in us will lead others to Him. It's going to light a fire under the uniqueness in us, the special set of gifts God hasn't given to anyone else. It's miraculous to think that each of us is created with a singular collection of God-selected abilities, all meant to be used for His glory, but we are, and opportunities to use them come every day.

Lord, thank You for the gifts You've given me for Your eternal purposes.

OCTOBER 13

If I ride the wings of the morning, if I dwell by the farthest oceans, even there Your hand will guide me, and Your strength will support me.
PSALM 139:9–10

In seasons when it feels quiet on the spiritual front, when it feels like God is distant from our needs and our hearts, He isn't. He never will be. There isn't a corner of the earth where we're out from under the cover of His love, nowhere far enough to escape His guiding hand. The strength of His love holds us—in the wilderness, on the mountaintop, and every step in between.

Father, You're with me in all seasons and every moment. Keep my heart strong and surrendered to Your purpose in all things.

Souls who follow their hearts thrive...
PROVERBS 13:19 THE MESSAGE

You have the favor of God on your life. Go for the life of your dreams! He sees your heart holding all the hopes you've had for so long, the things the child in you still imagines. He knit them into your being before you took your first breath. Don't give up believing He'll bring them to life.

Lord, You put desires in my heart for Your purposes and gave me the gifts to live them. I put my trust in You alone.

OCTOBER 15

With all my heart I want Your blessings...
PSALM 119:58 NLT

Love that forgives fast and forgets the past...
joy that bubbles from the inside out...peace
that brings a sense of calm all around...hope
that fills my words...kindness that shows I
care...compassion that moves me to action
and courage that makes me strong—these
are the blessings I want with all my heart, the
ones that make my heart like His.

Father, make my life a reflection of Your heart.

Surely Your goodness and unfailing love
will pursue me all the days of my life...
PSALM 23:6 NLT

It won't stop chasing us down, God's amazing goodness and unfailing love. We want it to overtake us today. We want it to roll over our souls like a wild, unexpected wave. It's going to wash away discouragement and sadness and refresh our world-weary hearts. It's what we want, God...so bring it on with all Your powerful, perfect heart.

Father, Your goodness and love are my joy and
strength. Thank You for giving them in abundance.

Those who are wise—the people of God—shall shine as brightly as the sun's brilliance, and those who turn many to righteousness will glitter the stars forever.
DANIEL 12:3 TLB

Be bold in your faith, be inspired by love, be the beautiful soul He created. You're gifted to do special things for the people your life touches. You're going to help them see what God's love looks like, what grace does to a heart, how *real* joy lights up a smile. It's all in you for your incredible purpose in Him…a purpose that's putting people on the path to eternity—and your life is pointing the way.

Father, make my heart tender toward Your purpose today and guide me by Your love.

Make me walk along the right paths,
for I know how delightful they really are.
PSALM 119:35 TLB

You're going to be brave today. You're going to dig deep into the truth of what God says about you and not spend a moment believing otherwise. You aren't what other people say about you, you aren't condemned for making a mistake, and you don't have to spend a minute feeling guilty before you feel forgiven. Be strong and believe—you are priceless...you are loved...you are whole...you are the joy of God's heart.

Father, I praise You for making me so
wonderfully unique, and I thank You
for loving me with all Your heart.

See how very much our Father loves us, for He
calls us His children, and that is what we are!…
I JOHN 3:1 NLT

Children put their complete trust in those
who care for them. They have a joy in them
that's so remarkable, so like the light of God's
presence. How does growing up challenge our
trust in our perfect Father and make our joy
so refrained? Today, let's ask Him to renew
our childlike trust and refresh the brightness
of that contagious joy sent straight from His
heart—and believe He'll be faithful to give it.

Father, Your joy is light and Your faithfulness
is true. Help me to walk in both today.

*...When your faith is tested, your endurance
has a chance to grow. So let it grow, for when
your endurance is fully developed, you will be
perfect and complete, needing nothing.*
JAMES 1:3–4 NLT

Our growth brings glory to God. It's all we
want, honestly, because it's all about leading
the hurting to Him, the hearts lost in the
harshness of living without His saving,
unconditional love. Can we imagine? We
don't want the easy path, unfamiliar with the
suffering of our Savior. We want the path that
helps us understand the cost of grace—and
realize what we go through can't come close
to the measure.

*Lord, I'll trust the shaping of my heart to
You. Make it more and more like Yours.*

*...Make the most of every
opportunity you have for doing good.*
EPHESIANS 5:16 TLB

They come and go every day, opportunities to do good. We might be tired from fighting our own doubts and fears, but love brings new energy. Love is good medicine—it makes happy hearts, it draws souls to the true Healer, and it makes every life feel valued. Pile it on today, the love and the good—and know it's making ripples in eternity.

Father, Your love is my inspiration and my joy. Give me every opportunity to show it.

The LORD is close to the brokenhearted; He
rescues those whose spirits are crushed.
PSALM 34:18 NLT

When life takes unexpected turns and loss breaks us into a million pieces, grief bears down. A life...a marriage...a job—suffering isn't selective. It comes to all of us in different ways, with more pain than any heart can measure—except One, who took the anguish of every sin and suffered the death that did not win. He paid for the grace that picks up every piece of us...and heals us to wholeness with love.

Lord, You are my hope and my Healer.
Thank You for the power of Your love.

*I'm an open book to You; even from a
distance You know what I'm thinking.*
PSALM 139:2 THE MESSAGE

If we think for a moment that God's not
thinking about us, we need to think again.
We aren't going to keep Him from loving us
today, no matter what we do. He's right here,
caring, carrying, strengthening, giving hope.
We are His—and He's not letting go.

*Father, Your love for me is constant and
unconditional. I'm never out of Your sight.*

...Through the death on the cross...Christ has brought you into the very presence of God, and you are standing there before Him with nothing left against you...
COLOSSIANS 1:22 TLB

Everything that happens in our lives is a direct effect of God's love, and its purpose is to put a floodlight on our need for Him. Some things humble, extracting fragments of pride we didn't realize were keeping parts of us from all of Him. It's always working good stuff in and bad stuff out, the refining love of God. It gives us an even clearer view of the cross and the One who carried it—the One who now carries us.

Lord, keep my heart and mind on Your immeasurable sacrifice and faithful love.

*You are merciful and gentle, Lord, slow in getting
angry, full of constant loving-kindness and of truth.*
PSALM 86:15 TLB

Today, let's be quick to love, quick to forgive,
and quick to be kind. Like our Father, let's be
slow to anger and filled with the truth: we are
light in this world, we are precious to God,
and He is more than enough—with grace
enough to be like Him.

Lord, give me grace to be Your love to the world.

The love of the LORD remains forever
with those who fear Him...
PSALM 103:17 NLT

Forever love. It's yours today, moment by God-filled moment. His heart is faithful to you, day and night, and your needs are never out of His sight. The worries trying to crowd in...He'll take each one and take care of what's causing them. All He wants from you is all-out trust that in every battle, He's all you need.

Lord, You're my tower of strength and my
Provider. All of my needs are met in You.

*Don't be discouraged...for the battle
is not yours, but God's.*
II CHRONICLES 20:15 NLT

We like to take part in our battles. They keep
us up at night and stand ready to face us in the
morning. But in *every* moment of *every* battle,
we're protected by the One who is on the
front line day and night—fighting for our win
without a closed eye or a turned shoulder.
God is at our defense and He doesn't fail—
and the end will always find us in His favor.

*Father, thank You that I am under Your watch and
beneath Your wings. You are my victory today.*

*...You are a guide...a light for people
who are lost in darkness.*
ROMANS 2:19 NLT

God moves things into place and brings people into our lives for His purposes. His love is for every heart. He wants the lost to be found, and we're the light that helps them see His love more clearly. The smallest act of kindness led by the greatest love of all can make all the difference in a life.

*Father, let Your light shine through me—
with kindness, love, and compassion.*

These trials are only to test your faith, to see
whether or not it is strong and pure...
I PETER 1:7 TLB

When questions fill our minds about the trials, here and heavy, we remind our weary hearts: if we didn't have the test, we wouldn't gain the trust. Easy journeys don't strengthen souls—the ones that God is preparing for greater things. We're not getting discouraged today, we're deciding to trust Him all the way through—and start getting excited about what He's going to do.

Father, I trust You with every moment
of the journey, knowing every step
brings me closer to You.

...He blesses the home of the righteous...
PROVERBS 3:33 THE MESSAGE

Lord, set our hearts on fire today and make Your love shine a little brighter on those around us. The ones who see us up close, the way You do...the hearts You've put under one roof...the ones we love the most. Your love is often sweetest here, and some days too trying. But You bless us and forgive us and help us forgive each other—and maybe that's the greatest blessing of all.

*Father, bless our homes—every heart
in them...and every heart that enters.*

...I am with you always, even to the end of the world.
MATTHEW 28:20 TLB

Today might bring more than we can handle, but God didn't design us to go it alone here. He's got the help we need and He'll *be* the strength we need. We'll draw hope from His grace and trust and listen. He's going to tell our hearts what to do... and He'll direct our steps in perfect order.

Father, thank You for being my ever-present help in every need.

*So let us come boldly to the very throne of
God and stay there to receive His mercy and to
find grace to help us in our times of need.*
HEBREWS 4:16 TLB

Staying right there, right where the mercy
is—that's how we start our days. Because
we can't go forward without finding the grace
we need. It's why we have hope and where we
know love. We leave our needs there, at His
throne, confident He'll take care of them.
It's as close as a prayer and the best place for
our opening moments today.

*Father, bold access to Your throne is beyond
my words. Thank You for making a way
through Jesus to be invited there.*

November 2

Be strong and of good courage, do not...
be afraid...for the LORD your God, He is the One
who goes with you. He will not leave you...
DEUTERONOMY 31:6 NKJV

You're strong in the Lord. You're the loved, valued, wonderfully created recipient of every blessing God gives. Nothing in this challenging, changing, uphill life can knock you far enough down to keep Him from lifting you up again. If fear comes, foil it with prayer. If stress presses in, breathe deep His peace. There's a courageous response to every curveball life throws—and every one of them is found in Him.

Lord, keep my heart at peace in
the blessings You give.

Therefore do not cast away your confidence,
which has great reward. For you have need
of endurance, so that after you have done the
will of God, you may receive the promise.
HEBREWS 10:35–36 NKJV

We can never, ever let our confidence in God
slip away. Not even for a moment. When
disappointment comes day after day and the
waiting wears us down, He's the only One
who can pull us up and move us forward.
Sadness will close in if we let it, but hope is
the most powerful antidote—and God has it
in endless supply.

Father, fill my heart with hope today.
My confidence is in You alone.

*He has showered down upon us the richness
of His grace—for how well He understands us
and knows what is best for us at all times.*

EPHESIANS 1:8 TLB

God's best will come in God's timing. Running ahead of Him will make the wait longer and the discouragement harder to defeat. God is so gracious and wise. He knows and understands us better than we do, and what we sometimes miss is the perfect and perfectly wonderful peace that comes with totally surrendering to His will for our lives.

*Lord, I know Your rich grace is sufficient every
day, as I wait in faith and surrender to Your will.*

I am always aware of Your unfailing love.
PSALM 26:3 NLT

Today we get another chance to live aware of God's constant love. How do we put our minds around the truth that no matter how many moments we live worried, afraid, impatient, or unloving—not a single thing can stop Him from loving us. God's love is as infinitely wonderful as we are in endless wonder of it. Give love away with all your heart today . . . *and begin with Him.*

Father, I love You with all my heart…and thank You for loving me with the beauty of Yours.

Examine me, GOD, from head to foot, order Your battery of tests. Make sure I'm fit inside and out.
PSALM 26:2 THE MESSAGE

We'll have all God wants for us if we're all-in for Him. All our trust in the promise that He's working everything together for good—because He is. All our joy in understanding that circumstances don't bring it—He does. All our heart and soul and mind loving Him—because He first loved us. God won't keep *any* good thing from getting to us…if we give Him all we are.

Father, help my heart surrender all to You.

Let your roots grow down into Him and
draw up nourishment from Him...
COLOSSIANS 2:7 TLB

He's nourishment for our hearts today—the truth that we're loved all the way through our moments, whether or not we make mistakes or get messy with our attitude or give voice to things better left unsaid. We're human and God remembers that we are. That why there's grace. And why, when our weaknesses win, it's so amazing.

Lord, You're the source of every goodness...and
the goodness of Your grace overwhelms me.

Will all your worries add a single moment to your life?
MATTHEW 6:27 TLB

Let's not spend our moments worrying today. We have to give everything to God for anything to go right. The beauty of it is, He wants the exchange—our worries for His peace. And that's the thing about God and grace—our hearts always win because He loves us so much.

Father, I lay my worries at Your feet and pick up the peace of Your love-filled promises.

Lord, be merciful to us, for we have waited
for You. Be our strong arm each day...
ISAIAH 33:2 NLT

The longer the wait, the more beautiful the outcome. His strong arm wins the battle and our hearts emerge stronger than ever. A strong heart creates a deeper faith, and nothing on earth brings more beauty to our lives than trusting God to do what He says He will do. So hold on if you're hoping today; something incredible is on the way.

Father, I wait for You with hope and patience.
You are my strength and my reward.

...Then you will know that I am the LORD.
Those who trust in Me will never be put to shame.
ISAIAH 49:23 NLT

God is paying attention to everything in your life and what you're going through. He's making provision for every single need you have. He's keeping promises because He loves you and His Word is truth. He's preparing you to finally see the hopes you've held long... watered with a thousand tears...and believed in with all your heart.

Father, You hold me in the palm of Your hand, and every hope I have is in You.

For I am always aware of Your unfailing love,
and I have lived according to Your truth.
PSALM 26:3 NLT

Spend some moments *aware* today. Notice
the sunrise and the cloud formations; look
long at the faces you love; think about how
good it feels to have a good friend. Note the
kindness of a stranger and those who smile
back. Sit thankful in the quiet at the end of
a day. Take time and you'll see the *always* of
God's unfailing love.

Father, open my eyes and my heart to see
Your unfailing love in all my days.

...You, O God, provided from Your goodness...
PSALM 68:10 NKJV

Maybe our hearts need peace today, after lying awake for too many hours, trying to push out thoughts of *There isn't enough* or *I don't have enough strength to get through.* Maybe we just need God's beyond-belief love to surround us like a shield. No matter what we need, God will provide it from His infinite goodness... in abundant measure.

Father, I trust in Your love and provision. Whatever my hearts needs, You're faithful to give it.

...Live carefree before God;
He is most careful with you.
I PETER 5:7 THE MESSAGE

God rejoices when we live carefree. It means our hearts are trusting fully in His care. He gives the tender promise that He's careful with us too. He's never harsh with our hearts or our lives. He knows we're in a harsh world, and He knows our frame; He remembers that we are dust. (See Psalm 103:14.) We can give our cares to Him and be happy because we're held by the most loving, careful hands.

Father, I put my cares in Your loving, careful
hands today and live joyfully in trust.

...I made you and I will care for you...
ISAIAH 46:4 TLB

There are gifts in giving God control. Peace comes...joy returns...hope emerges...and our hearts can rest. It's natural to want control, unnerving to let go—unless we put all into God's hands. He's so careful with us. He understands us...how we're wired...how hard it is for us to just trust. And so there's grace, reminding us of the sacrifice that made us whole, and we know that surrendering all is always best.

Father, You created me and care for me best.
Help me to put all things into Your hands.

...Love the LORD your God with all your heart,
with all your soul, and with all your mind.
MATTHEW 22:37 NKJV

All our hearts, every corner, every part...
filled with love for God. There's nothing
in this world that can make our lives more
radiant than being in love with God with
every ounce of our being. And no matter how
much we give, we'll never be able to reach the
magnitude or the measure of His love for us.

Father, Your love is my light
and the joy of my life.

> *...It's with lasting love that*
> *I'm tenderly caring for you.*
> ISAIAH 54:8 THE MESSAGE

God's love for you will never come to an end. It will never be altered by actions, never be marred by mistakes. His love for you comes with the most tender care and mercy you'll ever know, and it will never change. When life turns and bends and breaks you, you have God to hold you and keep you...with unchanging, unbreakable love.

Father, Your constant love is my hope and strength, and my life is in Your perfect care.

...I am with you; that is all you need...
II CORINTHIANS 12:9 TLB

It's often the ordinary things in life that shed light on the extraordinary God we serve. He's with us in the moments, and there are far more ordinary than extraordinary in our days. So we look for Him there. We invite Him in, talk to Him, and enjoy His presence. And when He answers our prayer for that simple, small thing, it lets us know we matter to Him...in an extraordinary way.

Lord, Your presence is my peace and joy.
I praise You for love that pays attention.

When you produce much fruit, you are my true disciples. This brings great glory to my Father.
JOHN 15:8 NLT

What God prunes in our lives He does with purpose, and He will always follow it with a greater harvest of good things than we ever thought possible. His love produces what's best for us, even if getting to His best takes a toll on our hearts—and sometimes it does. Pain can never be compared or minimized, but God is faithful to mend us. And stronger hearts, He knows, are best.

Father, I trust my life to You and my path to Your lead, knowing it will lead to Your best.

Our lives are a Christ-like fragrance rising up to God...
II CORINTHIANS 2:15 NLT

Every day is part of our journey to become more beautiful, *Christlike* beautiful, in the way we see others, treat others, and love others. Love makes our reflection radiant. It softens the edges of our attitudes and refines our ability to forgive quickly. Love brings out the best in us—and gives what's best to every life we touch.

Father, fill me to overflowing with Your love and let it pour out on others today.

*Let everything you say be good and
helpful, so that your words will be an
encouragement to those who hear them.*
EPHESIANS 4:29 NLT

Words are powerful. If we let God choose
each one we speak today, we'll speak kindness,
truth, and love into the lives of others. With
a simple encouragement, a heart in despair
might take away the hope they were looking
for; a heart broken might feel the comfort
needed. God, fill our words with grace and
goodness today.

*Father, let Your Spirit guide the words
I speak, and let me speak each one with love.*

*Be kind to each other, tenderhearted, forgiving one
another, just as God through Christ has forgiven you.*
EPHESIANS 4:32 NLT

Every kind thing we do makes some kind of difference. Our lives are busy and weighed down with all the things we think need to be done, when really all we need to do is love each other and be kind. God's got the rest. He's got our provision, our strength, and the plans that truly matter. So let's just trust Him so we can get busy being kind.

*Father, thank You for making me a vessel
of Your kind and loving heart.*

NOVEMBER 22

*...Let your light shine for all to see. For the
glory of the LORD rises to shine on you.*
ISAIAH 60:1 NLT

The vibrant, life-giving, breathtaking beauty
of our Lord is always with us—ready to
bring light...to give life...to draw others to
Him. It's a powerful privilege, carrying His
indescribable love within us—and our most
important purpose is to let it shine.

*Father, let the light of Your radiant love
shine through me into the lives of others.*

*Because of Christ and our faith in Him, we can now
come boldly and confidently into God's presence.*
EPHESIANS 3:12 NLT

God's presence…all light and love. Wouldn't
it be wonderful if that's what we brought
into the lives we touch—nothing negative or
unnecessary, just His light and His love. Maybe
we could do that today, and maybe God will do
some great things through us. We never know
how our lives will impact others, but we do
know His love makes an eternal difference.

*Lord, let Your life be the light and the
love that shines through me.*

You can make many plans, but the
LORD's purpose will prevail.
PROVERBS 19:21 NLT

Our plans fill up our days, and the days fly.
We pray, we hope, and we see God working
things together and letting things fall out
of place. But we can know if they do, it's in
line with His perfect purpose. No matter how
we prepare or plan or put things in places we
think they belong, God's purpose will always
prevail—and it will *always* be for the best.

Lord, Your will is the way that is loving and
best. Lead me into Your perfect purpose.

Whatever you do, do it with kindness and love.
I CORINTHIANS 16:14 TLB

The world needs love. Love is powered by God and promises change. It's always kind, never rude or abrupt. It's not impatient, but gentle, calm, and comforting. There's nothing that can weaken it and nothing that can ultimately win against it. There's darkness here, too much of it, and that's why our light makes all the difference. Be the light of God through kindness and love—and be sure that it's no small thing.

Father, Your love is best, and it makes a big difference every time it shines.

*...I am the LORD your God, who teaches
you what is good for you and leads you
along the paths you should follow.*
ISAIAH 48:17 NLT

God is in control of our lives. Each moment
holds purpose. Our steps are not random but
ordered, each one leading to where He wants
us to be. So right now, right this moment,
we are where we belong. We're not here by
chance, we're here to live fully and love fully—
to be content and confident in God's plan
for us.

*Lord, I trust the path of Your plan
and the love that guides it.*

Do not remember the former things, nor consider the
things of old. Behold, I will do a new thing...I will even
make a road in the wilderness and rivers in the desert.
ISAIAH 43:18—19 NKJV

God will make a way through the hard things we're facing, even if we can't see how. It might seem as if there's too much stacked against us and our hearts hang onto hope by a thread. But the wait is coming to an end. God is doing something new and incredibly good. We don't have to see *how* it will happen; we're in the hands of the One who's making it happen.

Father, I know You're watching and
working...and the wait is almost over.

I will bless the LORD who guides me...
PSALM 16:7 NLT

Our lives are guided by God's hand. Not a moment or a detail of what we go through is missed. There will be days that go wrong in too many ways, little things testing patience, sometimes bigger things stretching our faith muscles. God is right there with us, like the deep breaths we take...listening to the prayer we whisper...and at the ready to hear and to help.

Lord, thank You for being in every moment, to guide, strengthen, and answer.

...You have a glorious reputation because
of those never-to-be-forgotten deeds.
NEHEMIAH 9:10 TLB

The amazing things God has done—for us and in us—are clear reflections of His magnificent love. It's the unstoppable force that moved our hearts to surrender and fall in love with our Savior. It's the power in our prayers and the weapon against our fears. His love is what changed us and now challenges us to be better, do better, and love best—like Him—every single day.

Father, Your love is my rejoicing and
the greatest strength of my life.

*Through Christ, all the kindness of God
has been poured out upon us…*
ROMANS 1:5 TLB

We live to be poured out for God—to allow Him to create in us a pure heart, to be used for His purposes. He gave each of us special gifts for our journey, and He'll ignite them with passion. What we love to do—what sets our hearts aflame and gets us excited to be alive—is the given gift God will use for His glory.

*Lord, I give all my heart and all my gifts
to You for Your purpose and glory.*

Create in me a new, clean heart, O God.
Renew a loyal spirit within me.
PSALM 51:10 NLT

God's faithfulness to us is never in question. He's with us now, in all the tired bones of our bodies, to soothe our life-worn, weary hearts. He's here to make us new—to renew and refresh us with hope, strength, joy, whatever it is we need in this moment. And everything He gives is carefully covered in love.

Father, You're the comfort of my heart
and the strength of my days.

December 2

He is your praise and He is your God, the
One who has done mighty miracles...
DEUTERONOMY 10:21 TLB

Don't miss the miracles in the moment, His
presence everywhere, in every living thing.
God loves it when we pay attention, when we
see the wonder in all He's created. It keeps
us mindful of His constant presence, power,
and love. And it moves us to praise—that
sweet one-on-one time our hearts need and
His heart loves.

Father, You are the miracle in every living
thing, and my heart is filled with praise.

*...God never abandons us. We get knocked
down, but we get up again and keep going.*
II CORINTHIANS 4:9 TLB

God is aware of every breath and every
moment. He won't step away from being our
way through *any* storm. It rages, we rest—in
His love, faithfulness, and assurance that
He's got this. He'll still the winds and calm
the waters, and our hearts will come out of it
stronger than ever.

*Father, You're my strength through the
storm, on my way to becoming stronger.*

*All these new things are from God who brought us
back to Himself through what Christ Jesus did...*
II CORINTHIANS 5:18 TLB

If God brings an end to something in our
lives, we can believe, heart and soul, that it's a
gateway to better things than we can imagine.
He's moving us forward to His best and
what's best for us. God is present in our
moments and attending to the details. He
won't miss one. We're too important to Him,
too loved by Him, for anything that concerns
us to be overlooked.

*Father, I trust Your love for me and know that
every new thing You bring is a blessing.*

...All the powers of hell itself cannot keep
God's love away. Our fears for today,
our worries about tomorrow.
ROMANS 8:38 TLB

Fear can grip us some days, casting a shadow over the light of God's love, the love we know is true and powerful and present. God never leaves us, even when worries find their way in, leaving our hearts fearful. Let's be brave and let God's perfect love extinguish it. There's no room for it today, here in the hand that holds the universe, the hand that's holding us. There's only peace and perfect love.

Father, I'm at peace today in Your perfect
love—where fear has no place and no power.

DECEMBER 6

Be still, and know that I am God...
PSALM 46:10 NKJV

Being still keeps God moving in our lives. We trust He's doing what's best and putting our worries to rest. He loves us far too fully and faithfully to take us in any direction that isn't part of His plan for our lives—and it's all good.

Father, keep my heart at rest while
You lead me into Your best.

God is our refuge and strength,
a very present help in trouble.
PSALM 46:1 NKJV

We're not going to face anything today that can rob our peace. We have a secure refuge. We're not going to go through anything that can weaken our faith or lay waste to our hope. We have a present help, with the power to win. What we're going to do is rest in God every moment, being thankful to Him for being everything we need.

Father, You are always present and always faithful, with all I'll ever need.

DECEMBER 8

Your unfailing love will last forever. Your faithfulness is as enduring as the heavens.
PSALM 89:2 NLT

Live today fully and joyfully. Live like you're filled with the life-changing love of God—because you are. Let His more-than-your-heart-can-hold love overflow into actions motivated by compassion and words saturated with kindness and hope. Let love radiate from you in smiles that light up lives and hugs that give comfort. All love, all day...and all for God's glory.

Father, let Your love flow from me into every life I touch today.

It is good to proclaim Your unfailing love in the morning, Your faithfulness in the evening.
PSALM 92:2 NLT

The bookends of our day, Lord…Your love in the morning, Your faithfulness in the evening. All the moments in between awaken our awe of You and the work of Your hands in our lives…so constant, consistent, and loving. We can't thank You enough—for grace beyond belief and hope beyond measure.

Father, from beginning to end, Your love is the joy of my days.

December 10

...God doesn't want us to be shy with
His gifts, but bold and loving...
II TIMOTHY 1:7 THE MESSAGE

Let's love more boldly today—the unafraid, unconditional, unselfish way, when we don't care what we get out of it, we just want God in it. We want Him in all we do because that's when all kinds of good comes of it. And giving the gift of love is the best, most beautiful way to spend all our moments.

Father, help my heart to see the need,
and give me courage to love however You lead.

*Yet God has made everything beautiful for its own
time. He has planted eternity in the human heart...*
ECCLESIASTES 3:11 NLT

Our lives are beautiful because God lives in
us, and what shines out from us—and into the
world—are the eternal blessings He gives: His
everlasting joy that lights up our countenance
and doesn't change when circumstances do;
His endless hope that keeps us going when
things go wrong; and His infinite, invincible
love that changed our hearts...and through us
will change countless others.

*Father, You make my life beautiful with
the beauty of Your eternal blessings.*

DECEMBER 12

God is my strength and power, and
He makes my way perfect.
II SAMUEL 22:33 NKJV

We're as imperfect as God is perfect, and still
He makes our way perfect. He doesn't see our
flaws; He sees the pierced hands that cover
them in grace. Nothing is held against us
now; our sins were held to the cross by nails
that will never deteriorate. We stand in the
strength of our Savior, to walk in the way of
His perfect love.

Lord, You light my path with the glory
of grace. Help me to mark each step
with the light of Your love.

LORD, You have heard the desire of the humble; You will prepare their heart; You will cause Your ear to hear.
PSALM 10:17 NKJV

God, make Your desires our joy today, and remind us again that You alone give us the strength and power to fulfill them. Anything good in us is from Your life in us. Grace gets us through our days and past our own desires to *Your* desires. They're the only ones that make a loving, lasting difference in the world.

Lord, help me surrender my desires to Yours with a thankful heart.

Now you have every grace and blessing; every
spiritual gift and power for doing His will...
1 CORINTHIANS 1:7 TLB

One day at a time—that's the pace of grace.
There's no grace for what may be and no
peace in worrying about what's to come.
There's grace for what *is*. God wants us to be
in the moment with Him, where He meets
our need and opens our eyes to His purpose
in the place we're in. He brought us here and
it's where we belong.

Father, help me keep my focus on
You and the moment I'm in.

*...See that you go on growing in the Lord, and
become strong and vigorous in the truth...*
COLOSSIANS 2:7 TLB

Our growth in God should be our deepest
desire. We'll never be able to fully know Him
or genuinely grasp the magnitude of grace.
But we can keep trying, keep being amazed,
keep pulling Him closer. The best part of
growing in Him is becoming more like Him,
so let's get strong in the truth and stronger
in Him and put a lot more love in the world.

*Father, give me a clearer view of You and
a deeper understanding of truth so that I
can be a brighter reflection of You.*

Three things will last forever—faith, hope,
and love—and the greatest of these is love.
1 CORINTHIANS 13:13 NLT

At the root of every good thing is God's love. It's more vast than the universe and deeper than any ocean—and it's as good as it is fathomless. His love for us isn't moved by emotion; it's secured by grace. And it's rock-solid. Nothing you've done and not a thing you do can keep Him from raining down on you with His remarkable, unrelenting love.

Father, thank You for loving me and for pouring
Your love through me into the lives of others.

...His love is the wonder of the world...
PSALM 31:21 THE MESSAGE

A life filled with childlike wonder is a life
filled with God. His love keeps our eyes open
to the beauty and mystery of the world around
us. It helps us to stay curious and teachable.
And it gives us an incandescent joy that lights
up the lives of others.

*Father, Your love brings amazement and
wonder to the moments of our lives.*

Let love be your highest goal!...
I CORINTHIANS 14:1 NLT

Don't let the day go by without being God's love to someone. He'll open opportunities and lead others to you if your heart is willing to give, because His love gives *life*. So many discouraged and hurting souls cross our paths every day, and only God knows their true and deepest needs—and the truest need in all of us is love.

Lord, lead me by Your grace to those who need You most.

O Lord, I will honor and praise Your name, for You are my God; You do such wonderful things!...
ISAIAH 25:1 TLB

If you're trusting God to open a new door... if you need provision for something you weren't prepared for...if there's a hope deep down that you've never spoken...watch and see the wonderful things He'll do. You matter to Him more than you'll ever know—and His love for you is bringing things to pass that you can't imagine.

Lord, all the things I hope for are in Your hands. I trust them to Your timing and love.

*From His abundance, we have all received
one gracious blessing after another.*
JOHN 1:16 NLT

Everything by grace: all we are now, all we hope to become, and all that He gives so abundantly. By way of grace, our blessings are not limited, they come to us day after day, one right after another. Jesus came to give His life for it, and there's nothing on earth or in the heavens that can equal it, earn it, or exempt us from receiving it in infinite measure.

*Lord, we thank You and praise You for every
ounce of grace given so freely. Your love for us
goes beyond any measure our hearts can fathom.*

The counsel of the LORD stands forever,
the plans of His heart to all generations.

PSALM 33:11 NKJV

Our plans for the day are subject to change,
always, by the One whose counsel stands first
and forever. If we surrender our moments to
God, God will guide our steps, and our hearts
will be able to take each one with grace—and
trust where they lead with joy.

Father, I'll follow Your plans joyfully
and trust You with all my heart.

*So teach us to number our days, that
we may gain a heart of wisdom.*
PSALM 90:12 NKJV

Every moment of every day is monumental.
"Our days are few and brief, like grass, like
flowers" (Psalm 103:15 TLB). We need to ask
God to help us cherish each one and every
person in them. Lives are put together for a
reason, and it's *His* reason. He sees the heart—
not the outside—and that's why loving one
another takes God to show us how.

*Father, give me the grace and the wisdom
to love better and cherish the moments.*

Your word is a lamp to my feet and a light to my path.
PSALM 119:105 NKJV

Our path might be washed away by pelting storms of things not happening as soon as we hoped and losing relationships we felt we needed most, but what we need most, what matters most of all, is the Lord getting close to our broken hearts and saying, "I am the One that even the wind and the waves obey." His words are *light* that covers our path with hope and love that never fails.

Lord, I trust Your Word to light my path
and fill my heart with new hope.

DECEMBER 24

Now hope does not disappoint, because the
love of God has been poured out in our hearts
by the Holy Spirit who was given to us.
ROMANS 5:5 NKJV

Hope keeps the heart open to possibility, steady through change, and courageous in challenges. It stands on faith, the strongest foundation of all. Nothing can cause it to crumble or shake us from it. We hold fast, because we know it comes from the One who never fails.

Father, praise You for the hope
that keeps our hearts strong.

DECEMBER 25

You shall name Him Jesus (meaning "Savior"),
for He will save His people from their sins.
MATTHEW 1:21 TLB

He's the love of our lives because He surrendered His life out of staggering love for
us. He was born to die and chose to be.
Love doesn't get any deeper, wider, higher,
or more astounding than that. Let's spend
some moments today—maybe a lot of them—
remembering why He came and rejoicing that
He did.

Lord, my heart is overwhelmed by the love
that brought You here—and now brings
us grace and the gift of eternal life.

The LORD directs the steps of the godly…
PSALM 37:23 NLT

God has you on a unique path. The gifts He's
put in you will be engaged, the traits you have
will be shaped for His glory, and there will
be people along the way who need the love
in your heart in a way only you can give it.
They'll see the likeness of your Father in you,
and that's the most beautiful part of the plan.

*Lord, direct my steps, teach my heart, and
make me more and more like You.*

Always be full of joy in the Lord;
I say it again, rejoice!
PHILIPPIANS 4:4 TLB

Let's start our day full of joy, before lists come out and routine rushes in. Let's take a moment to smile, for no reason other than to feel it spread sunshine across our face. Let's think about something that made us laugh, and laugh all over again. Positive and negative thoughts are choices...and sometimes feelings are too. Let's choose the high road and the most high God today. It'll keep our hearts filled with joy.

Lord, walk with me today,
and help me to see the joy that
You bring to the little things.

December 28

Show me Your strong love in wonderful ways, O Savior of all…
PSALM 17:7 TLB

Show us Your strong love today, Lord, when things are going wrong and we feel like we haven't done very many things right. Remind us of Your wonderful peace and the wonders of Your grace. Help us to stay encouraged by the sky-reaching faithfulness of Your love when we get discouraged by the struggle we're in. Your love for us is never interrupted—not even for a moment—and it's the strength of all our days.

Father, let Your love be my strong tower and constant comfort today.

*...Is that a joyous choir I hear? No, it is the Lord
himself exulting over you in happy song...*
ZEPHANIAH 3:18 TLB

You're divinely created and celebrated every
day of your life. Your name is written on the
palm of God's hand and you're never out of
His thoughts. He knows the details of your
day and the purposes of your life. Today, take
a few moments to reflect on the joy He has
in you, and show Him all the love you have
for Him.

*Father, Your love makes me happy...
and Your joy in me overjoyed.*

DECEMBER 30

Live in Me. Make your home in Me just as I do in you...
JOHN 15:4 THE MESSAGE

In God, there is absolutely, inarguably no place like home. He's the comfort we need at the end of every day, the love we need without condition or expectation, the quiet rest away from the world. He's our refuge, our place to refuel, and the place we're truly known and always accepted. Father, we *will* make our home in You today...and welcome You wholeheartedly into ours.

Lord, live in me and fulfill Your purposes.
There's nothing in this world that
can take the place of You.

...I have formed you, you are My servant...
you will not be forgotten by Me!
ISAIAH 44:21 NKJV

God never leaves you, and He never loses sight of what He created you to do. You are in His thoughts, engraved on His hand, and surrounded by His love. What matters to you matters to Him, and there's no one on earth who can take your place. His purposes for you will come to pass, with perfect love, at the perfect time.

Father, all that I am is surrendered to You.

LIVE YOUR FAITH

Dear Friend,

This book was prayerfully crafted with you, the reader, in mind—every word, every sentence, every page—was thoughtfully written, designed, and packaged to encourage you...right where you are this very moment. At DaySpring, our vision is to see every person experience the life-changing message of God's love. So, as we worked through rough drafts, design changes, edits, and details, we prayed for you to deeply experience His unfailing love, indescribable peace, and pure joy. It is our sincere hope that through these Truth-filled pages your heart will be blessed, knowing that God cares about you—your desires and disappointments, your challenges and dreams.

He knows. He cares. He loves you unconditionally.

BLESSINGS!
THE DAYSPRING BOOK TEAM

Additional copies of this book and
other DaySpring titles can be purchased
at fine bookstores everywhere.
Order online at <u>dayspring.com</u>
or
by phone at 1-877-751-4347